CW01506564

A FOUNTAIN
OF HOPE

❈❈❈❈❈❈❈❈

ALVAN IBEH, SMMM

V e r b u m
Publications
Published by Verbum Publications

ISBN:

978-0-9929573-9-1

First edition published 2024 Printed in the UK

*****

Cover and interior design by Designed4Print

Dedication

I dedicate this book to the loving memories of my beloved friend and big brother, Late Rev Fr Abel Ezenwa.
May your gentle soul continue to rest in the peace of Christ.

* * * * * *

Acknowledgements

My thanks to all who have helped in contributing to this book

Particular acknowledgements to individuals as referenced in the book for their contribution:

Joyce Meyer, Amy Collette, Denis Waitley, Willie Nelson, Cynthia Ozick, William Earnhardt: *They Called Her a Whore, Jesus Called Her a Woman'* Ashley Ballou-Bonnema, American-based gospel singer, Sinach, Debbie Przybylski, Eleanor Roosevelt, Kim Thompson Pinder: *'Your gift will make room for you – Proverbs 18:16 Explained'* published at *Faithisland.org.* Kelli Mahoney, Simon Heighweya, Michelle Cruz-Rosado, Israelmore Ayivor: *The Great Handbook of Quotes,* Grace Houle, Lisa Jones, Joel Osteen, Kate Prain, Eric Thomas, Bill Hybels, David Strain: '*I shall come forth as Gold',* Connie Rowland: '*You are God's, Masterpiece*' Daily Reflection: Produced by *The High Callin,* Tom Goymour: Foreword

Organisations:
Anon, True stories Re-told, London: Evangelical union of South America,
www.pictureQuotes.com, Christianstt.com, Application Bible, Jerusalem Bible,
www.Knowing Jesus.com, www.Lords-prayer-words.com

I wish to thank Tom Goymour (Verbum Publications) for his hard work in making this dream come true.
I also thank Dorothy Miller and other friends who gave me so much encouragement to complete this work. I remain ever grateful to you all.

Biblical scripture references:

Unless otherwise stated the references refer to the New International Version of the bible (NIV). Where other versions are quoted the appropriate citation has been given in the same form:
King James Version (KJV), English Standard Version (ESV)

Foreword

For most, faith is a journey, and, like any journey, before we travel, we need to be sure we know where we are going and that we can make it there safely with the best possible experience. But it's not always easy – even when we have planned carefully and think we know the route, there are always obstacles in the way: traffic jams, diversions, weather conditions, our health – unexpected interruptions can always cause us to reconsider our plans. Sometimes we might even question whether we really need to make that journey in the first place!

When things don't go according to plan, often the best we can do is hope. Hope is a wonderful positive human emotion. But hope needs to be based on real belief. A driver who runs low on fuel but planned his route on minor isolated roads hasn't given himself the best chance; a traveller on foot who didn't take any water to a baron place on a hot day is asking for trouble, but it doesn't mean there is no hope. With faith in God there is always hope and during our journey of faith, just like the practical equivalent in our day-to-day lives, there is always a way to overcome the obstacles life throws at us.

In these pages a **Fountain of Hope** awaits you, because just like as is needed for any expedition, faith requires some navigation. Although we are not all at the same point of travel, we all need to know the way.

What is particularly powerful about this book is the way in which every chapter has been written with clarity, showing us how and why the subject affects our relationship with God, the problems we may encounter and what we should do about it. A glance at the chapter headings alone can give you an insight into how this book approaches these issues.

Written from personal experience and following a journey that shows how he lives life championing hope as a real cusp of faith, the author has captured an engaging way of getting the message across that is easy to relate to.

There is a fountain of hope within all of us, you just need to know how to find it. The following pages will certainly guide you well.

Tom Goymour: Verbum Publications

Contents

Introduction

Many things happening around us today can easily cause us to lose our taste for life, but our hope in God keeps us going even when the storms around us become so strong that we do not know what to do anymore.

To hope is to have the conviction that even though what we are asking for is not yet here, one day it surely will be. Or hope is not in things of this world, it is in God, who never changes. In other words, this is a hope that is truly reassuring beyond anything else that we can know.

St Paul wrote in Romans 5:5,

'And hope does not put us to shame, because God's love has been poured into our hearts through the Holy Spirit, who has been given to us.' (NIV)

The New Living Translation puts it slightly differently

'And this hope will not lead to disappointment. For we know how dearly God loves us, because he has given us the Holy Spirit to fill our hearts with his love.'

We place our hope in God because we are convinced of the immensity of His love for us, and we are fully aware that He never disappoints those who hope in Him. I have experienced this and have come to believe beyond any doubt that it is true. It is that firm belief that is behind all the content in the chapters of this book.

This book is a compilation of some of the articles I wrote for the newsletter of my former parish in Bury St Edmunds, England, and I am indebted to some of the wonderful parishioners for giving me the encouragement to compile those articles into a book. I pray that as you read through these pages, your hope in God will be greatly strengthened and you will find a sure reason to continue to hope in Him no matter how difficult or impossible any situation or problem may seem. For God, all things are possible.

1
God is Never Late

When you are invited to have a meal with friends or family, as you enter their homes you are greeted by fine aromas emanating from the kitchen. The good smells make you look forward to eating what they have prepared. Similarly, I have chosen the title of this first chapter to whet your appetite and encourage you to keep reading to the end without getting bored. So, I begin this book by telling you that God is never, and has never been late.

Have you ever been late for an occasion before? What if you were expecting someone for an important event where they were supposed to arrive on time but disappointingly turned up late? Imagine how you would feel.

Let us make it more practical: Imagine your loved one suddenly becomes terribly ill to the point of losing consciousness. They need resuscitation and an emergency ambulance to quickly take them to hospital. When you call for an ambulance, you are told that one is on its way. You wait and wait but there is no sign of it. Your loved one is deteriorating fast, and it seems like no help is forthcoming. Then the telephone rings, it is a call from the ambulance service,

"Hello sir/madam, we are so sorry, but we have been held up in heavy traffic because of a fatal accident. The police are trying to make a way through for us, we are not sure how long it will take us to get to you, but we will be there as soon as we can."

They tried their best to get to you, but by the time they arrived, it was too late, your loved one had died. Imagine how you would feel about this whole scenario. Your loved one would have survived if they had arrived sooner? Depending on your level of understanding, you may want to put all the blame on the ambulance service for not arriving early enough and believe that they had left your loved one to die. Because emotions would be running high at that point, you may not understand that the paramedics had tried their absolute best but because of circumstances beyond their control, they were not able to make it on time.

If this type of thing has happened to you before, then you will appreciate even more the feelings of Mary and Martha, when they lost their beloved brother Lazarus. The story is recorded in John 11: 1-45: Lazarus was an exceptionally good friend of Jesus. I think they must have been so close that the very first thing Jesus would have done on hearing the news about his sickness would be to leave everything He was doing and rush straight down to the house of Lazarus to see him and save him from dying. But there was no need to panic because Jesus was aware of His power over death. Lateness is not in His dictionary. He knew that whatever time He arrived would be the right and appropriate time for Him to be there. He is always on time, even when people think otherwise. He is never late.

'So, the sisters sent word to Jesus, "Lord, the one you love is sick"'

(John 11:3)

He was very calm. All He had to say was,

'This sickness will not end in death. No, it is for God's glory, so that God's son may be glorified through it.'

(John 11:4)

Is there anything Jesus is trying to teach us here? Yes, of course. Jesus did not start panicking and running up and down. Because He knew of His power over death, He remained calm. He saw what the people could not see, that even though Lazarus was going to die, He would raise him from the dead by His almighty power, thereby teaching His flock and giving glory to God.

Now, scripture records that Jesus after receiving the news about the sickness of His friend, did not rush down to see him immediately, rather He stayed two days before getting to them. Verses 5 and 6 of John 11 report,

'Jesus loved Martha and her sister and Lazarus. Yet when he heard that Lazarus was sick, he stayed where he was two

more days.'

In our ordinary way of thinking, we would have said that Jesus was not actually a good friend to these people. Why did He not hurry to get there before His friend Lazarus died? This is exactly the way we make our conclusions when we find ourselves in similar circumstances. We ask God a lot of questions angrily –

"God, I have prayed so long for this particular problem, but you kept quiet, now it's too late!" But the question is, can anything be too late for God? Can God ever be late? If we understand the true nature of God, then we know that the answer is NO. God does not see things the way we see them. What we see as late, for Him is still exceedingly early. Of course, God is not limited by time. He works on a completely different time scale from ours. It is when we think all hope is lost and nothing more can be done, that we think He is too late. But that is when we hear Him knock at our door! He does not come to apologise for being late or to sympathise with us. He comes to make a difference. He comes to change our story.

From the story of Lazarus, Jesus intentionally decided to delay getting there, knowing that by the time He got there it would be too late. So, what was His reason for delaying? He gives the answer in John 11:14,

> **'So, then He told them plainly, "Lazarus is dead, and for your sake I am glad I was not there, so that you may believe. But let us go to him.'**

If Jesus had been with Lazarus during the decisive moments of Lazarus's sickness, he might have healed him rather than let him die, but Lazarus died so that Jesus' power over death could be shown to his disciples and others. The raising of Lazarus was an essential display of his power, and resurrection from the dead is a crucial belief in the Christian faith.

Jesus not only raised Himself from the dead, but he has power to raise others. He has the power to change every situation no matter how bad it is, but He wants us to believe in His power.

Believe that nothing is too hard for Him to do.

Believe that He can never be late.

Even when things do not go the way we want, we still need to believe that God has a plan for us and His plan is perfect.

When we are down to nothing, God is up to something

I can remember when I prayed fervently for the healing of my fractured hand, for the sole reason of going back to school to join my classmates. My prayer was answered, but not in the way I wanted. God answered it in His own way and in His own time. In the end I missed my classmates, but God had a better plan. When we pray, we should be asking God to do His will in our lives and not for our will to be done.

When Jesus finally got to His friend's house, He was told that He had been dead for four days and would now smell. The different comments from people show that all hope is lost and nothing else can be done about Lazarus's death. Martha said,

'Lord, if you had been here, my brother would not have died.'

Mary said the same thing. The Jews said,

'See how he loved him.'

But some of the Jews said,

'Could not he who opened the eyes of the blind man have kept this man from dying?'

When Jesus got to the tomb, He told them to,

'Take away the stone.'

Martha said,

'But, Lord, by this time there will be a bad odour, for he has been there four days.'

Martha's response shows that she believes it is too late for Jesus to do anything at that point in time. It does not matter how long He has stayed in the Tomb. It does not matter how long death has been holding him captive. What matters is that the Master has arrived. The one that gives and takes life has arrived on the scene. The scripture says He holds the key to life. All who believe will have life, John 3:16 and He has come so that we may have this life abundantly. John 10:10. Jesus told Martha, "

'Did I not tell you that if you believe, you will see the glory of God?'

After that He prayed to His Father and in a loud voice, He called out to Lazarus,

'Lazarus come out!'

In my own words,

"Lazarus, hear the voice of the giver of life and receive your breath back."

'And when the one who was dead heard this voice, He woke from his sleep and came forth.'

Then Jesus said,

'Unbind him and let him go.'

This whole drama ended immediately the Master arrived.

You may have experienced a situation when you prayed seriously for something and just when you thought it was too late and you were about to give up praying for it, you received an answer to your prayers. If we say God is never late, we mean that there will not be a time when we will tire of waiting for him. To believe in him means to continue to wait even when it looks like no answer is coming our way. Even if we feel He is delaying in answering our prayers, He is just sorting things out for us and if we patiently wait for Him, all things will work out for our good in the end, (Romans 8:28), but we need to be mindful of the fact that God will not explain to us why things happen the way they do. But when everything has taken place according to His plans, we will understand.

'We often say God is never late, but generally, He is not early either. Why? Because He uses times of waiting to stretch our faith in Him and to bring about change and growth in our lives'.

(Joyce Meyer)

I will end this chapter with a few testimonies from various sources. Testimonies are powerful, they can change lives unexpectedly. The first is from an anonymous person and is taken from the book *True Stories Re-told.*

'Life for Dona Rita – a poor Argentine woman, was exceedingly difficult, and the future appeared dark indeed. Her husband was becoming increasingly addicted to drink, and consequently, all the money he earned found its way into the tavern at the corner of the street. The burden of feeding and clothing the family of growing children had therefore to be carried by their mother, who spent long hours at the washtub. But the family was numerous, and the money so hardly earned was not sufficient, so the children were often cold and hungry. But things were to become even worse, for the husband began to insist that some of the money that his wife earned be given over to him. Dona Rita became desperate, for the future seemed absolutely bleak, without a ray of light. To struggle anymore was useless. Thus, it was that she decided upon a very terrible step: since life was no longer worth living, she would put an end to the suffering both for herself and the children. That surely would be better than living in increasing misery. She secured some poison and mixed it with the rice she and the unsuspecting children were to take for their midday meal.

But human extremity often proves God's opportunity. The meal was about to be served when there came a knock at the door, and a neighbour asked:

"Dona Rita, what are you doing this afternoon?"

"Why do you ask?" stammered the woman, thinking that her dreadful secret had in some way been discovered.

"I have come to invite you to a Gospel meeting!"

"What kind of meeting is that?" inquired Dona Rita.

"Oh, it is where someone speaks about God and the Lord Jesus Christ and His death on the cross. The meeting only lasts an hour, and I am sure you would enjoy it"

Conflicting thoughts chased one another through Dona Rita's mind. If she carried out her plan, she and her family would all be dead by the time of the meeting. But the mention of God made her reflect that after all she was taking a wrong step. Little guessing what her thoughts were, but seeing her hesitation, the neighbour again insisted,

"Do say you will come. I will call for you at 4 o'clock and we can go together".

"Yes, I will come," she promised; and she meant it.

Immediately the neighbour had gone, the poisoned food was thrown away and something else was hastily prepared. In the afternoon, Dona Rita went to the meeting and heard things quite new to her which amazed her and made her become so anxious to hear more. Before many weeks had passed, she had accepted Christ as saviour and friend. Life for her changed completely, she no longer had to bear her heavy load alone. She sent her children to Sunday school where they learnt that God hears and answers prayer. One day, as they gathered to pray, her little daughter said, "Mother, let's ask God to change father." They prayed for their father that night. The prayer was answered. A preacher visited their home the next day to ask him to attend their services, and although he never accepted the invitation, He did leave off drinking.

Some years have passed since Dona Rita accepted the saviour, and while her husband has not yet taken the same step, several of her children have. She has also had the joy of seeing a nephew whom she brought to Sunday school accept Christ as saviour.'

(Anon, True stories Re-told, London: Evangelical union of South America, 1965, Pages 13,14).

I have witnessed the testimony of a couple who were married for 18 years without having a single child. People in my culture believe that every married woman must give her husband children.

If this does not happen, the woman suffers a lot from bad comments from people, who may sometimes unkindly accuse her of being barren. But of course, it may not be the woman who has the fertility problem but the man. The couple I am talking about here experienced this. According to the man, at one point there was serious pressure from his family to marry a new wife. But he refused and stood by his wife while they waited on the Lord. They took tests to affirm that they were medically okay. They kept seeking God's face and waiting upon Him, because they were aware that those who wait upon the Lord can never be disappointed. After 18 long years of waiting and enduring accusations and name-calling, God arrived and put all the woman's accusers to shame. God blessed them not just with one child but with triplets! They trusted firmly in God and He turned their sadness to joy, their weeping to rejoicing, and their sorrow to dancing. The God of surprises surprised them and rewarded them for their trust in Him.

Keep trusting God.

'For the Lord will vindicate His people and have compassion on His servants. God stands up for his people; God holds the hands of his people.'

(Psalm 135:14)

We need to remain dependent on God and look to Him to vindicate us. When things are not working out as we wish, we must remain patient and keep waiting for God because he is worth waiting for. He is never late one bit. We need to stop trying to move ahead of God. His timing is perfect. Let us ask him therefore to give us the grace to always trust Him completely, knowing full well that He is never late, but always right on time. God has his own sense of timing:

'...with the Lord one day is as a thousand years and a thousand years as one day.'

(2 Peter 3:8)

He has perfect timing: never early, never late. God is never in a hurry, but he is always on time.

Prayer:

Help me Lord to be still in Your presence and to wait quietly and patiently before You my God, as did the Psalmist. Many and precious are the promises You have given to Your children, and I desire to rest in them by faith and to abide in You moment by moment, to the praise of Your holy name.

I thank You Lord that You hear all the prayers of Your children and that before we call, you have promised to answer. I also thank You that You are teaching me specifically that even though the answer may be long in coming, through it, you are developing in me a patient trust in You and establishing an even firmer faith in Your word – for Your word is true and You are a faithful and merciful God.

Thank You Lord that Your Word is becoming more deeply rooted within my heart and I pray that I will not faint when answers are delayed, but rather that I will quietly and patiently rest in Your unfailing promises as Your Holy Spirit does His work within my heart. Increase my love and dependence upon You so that I may become more like the Lord Jesus in every area of my life – so that I may bear much fruit, to Your praise and glory.

Amen

2
Learn to be Grateful for All Things

In life, we often find ourselves complaining about one thing or the other. Sometimes we complain about what we have, forgetting that there are some people out there who may desperately need to have the very thing we are complaining about. Other times we complain about what we do not have. The more we complain and moan about what we lack, the more impossible it becomes for us to see and be grateful for what we do have. There is a very apt saying where I come from -

'When we are ungrateful, we become great fools and when we are thankful, our tank will be full.'

One of the secrets of lasting happiness is to learn to be thankful to God no matter what situation we find ourselves in. We were not born with this attitude, but it's something we can learn. When we discover this secret of lasting happiness, we will experience a great turnaround in our lives. A constantly grateful heart is a constantly happy heart. This is why Amy Collette says,

'Gratitude is a powerful catalyst for happiness. It's the spark that lights a fire of joy in your soul.'

Denis Waitley has this to say,

'Happiness cannot be travelled to, owned, earned, worn or consumed. Happiness is the spiritual experience of living every minute with love, grace and gratitude.'

To be grateful in all things is to be contented in all things, whatever the situation, condition or circumstance life throws at us.

St Paul in his letter to the Philippians (4:2) says,

'I know what it is to be in need, and I know what it is to have plenty. I have learned the secret of being content in any and every situation, whether well fed or hungry,

whether living in plenty or in want.'

Paul was content because he tried his best to see life from God's point of view. He focused on what he was supposed to do not what he felt he should have. He had his priorities straight, and he was grateful for everything God had given him. Ordinarily, he would have been full of complaints and grumbling because of all he was going through following his conversion. Often in trouble, Paul was confronted, jailed (though angels rescued him), physically abused, repeatedly endangered, and harassed for preaching the very message that he previously attacked himself. Despite all the dangers he encountered, Paul's trust in God never wavered. In the same letter to the Philippians (4:6) he wrote,

'Do not be anxious about anything, but in everything by prayer and petition, with thanksgiving, present your requests to God.'

Imagine never being anxious about anything! It seems like an impossible dream, because we all have worries in our work, our homes, at school, etc. We always have one thing or another to complain about. But Paul's advice is to turn our worries into prayers. The more we worry, the more we are likely to complain. The more we complain, the more difficult it will be for us to see a reason to be grateful to God. So, we must complain less and thank God more.

We must learn to count our blessings every day. It is only when we sit down and start to think of all we have, or rather have received, (of course there is nothing we have that we have not received), that it will be clear to us that God deserves our praise, honour, and thanksgiving.

This will change our lives for the good.

Willie Nelson says:

'When I started counting my blessings, my whole life turned around.'

There is an old song that says,

'Count your blessings, name them one by one, count your blessings see what God has done, count your blessings, name them one by one, and it will surprise you what the Lord has done.'

There are indeed so many blessings which God out of His love has lavished upon us, both physical and spiritual blessings.

'Praise be to the God and Father our Lord Jesus Christ, who has blessed us in the heavenly realms with every spiritual blessing in Christ.

(Ephesians 1:3)

The greatest gift we have received from God is that of His Son Jesus Christ, who gave His life for us all to live. Yet, we very often forget this great gift, this great blessing which is beyond any other thing we could ask for! When did you last make time to thank God, not for any other thing but just for life?

'We often take for granted the very things that most deserve our gratitude.'

The words of Cynthia Ozick:

We must not fail to show our appreciation to God for this beautiful and perfect gift He has given to us. If I see life as a gift, then there won't be any reason for me to start thinking of taking my life. If I did, I would be like someone who received a gift and then not feeling grateful enough, decided to throw it away. If only we would remain ever grateful to the giver of this gift, and patiently unwrap it, we would discover how beautiful and perfect it is. When a wrapped gift is given to me, I will first and foremost be grateful to the giver. Then I will with great anticipation patiently unwrap the gift until I discover the content of the box. Sometimes, it may not be something that I may love, but I still need to be grateful because it has been given out of love.

We still need to be grateful to God no matter what we receive from Him, because He knows what is best for us. He knows what we need more than we do and all He gives us is beautiful.

'**"For I know the plans I have for you," declares the Lord**, **"plans to prosper you and not to harm you, plans to give you hope and a future."'**

(Jeremiah 29:11)

'The worth and meaning of a gift do not come from the size of the box, its monetary value, or even the ribbon that adorns it. Its meaning comes from how it makes you feel inside as the giver. The greatest gifts are not boxes filled with things, but beautiful presents that hold so much more: love, kindness, selflessness, and gratitude. They all make up the beautiful gift of life.'

(Ashley Ballou-Bonnema)

I want to share this touching story with you:

There was a blind girl who hated herself because she was blind. She hated everyone, except her loving boyfriend. He was always there for her. She told her boyfriend,

"If I could only see the world, I would marry you." One day, someone donated a pair of eyes to her, when the bandages came off, she was able to see everything, including her boyfriend.

He asked her

"Now that you can see the world, will you marry me?"

The girl looked at her boyfriend and saw that he was blind. The sight of his closed eyelids shocked her. She hadn't expected that. The thought of looking at them for the rest of her life led her to refuse to marry him.

Her boyfriend left her in tears and days later wrote a note to her saying: 'Take good care of your eyes, my dear; for before they

23

were yours, they were mine.'

This is exactly how the human brain often works when our status changes. Only a very few remember what life was like before, and who was always by their side in the most painful situations.

It is very important to always remember that life is a gift. Today, before you say any careless words, spare a thought for someone who is unable to speak. Appreciate God for the gift of speech and let words that come from your mouth be those that will give glory to God and edify those who listen to you. Don't be drawn to say hurtful things that might break the hearts of others. Allow your words to bring smiles to the faces of your listeners.

Before you complain about the taste of your food, think of someone who has nothing to eat. Whenever you have something to eat, give thanks to God for it. It is only when you experience days without any hope of having food that you will appreciate the food you are eating now, even if it is tasteless. There was a prayer before meals we said in the form of a song, during my nursery school days and it goes like this:

'Some have food but cannot eat, some can eat but have no food, we have food, and we can eat, glory be to you Oh God. Amen.'

I didn't realise the true meaning then, but now I have come to appreciate the beauty of this lovely prayer. Some have food but they can't eat, think about people who are sick; some have been asked by the doctor to stop eating anything called food because of their diagnosis. You can imagine how it feels, seeing others enjoying their meals but you are not allowed to enjoy with them. You can only eat with your eyes and not with your mouth. This seems like punishment. I can remember how I felt when I was asked to stop eating the two things I enjoy most, because of ill health. I wasn't myself for almost two months and couldn't wait to be allowed to start eating them again.

Some people can eat, have very good appetites, but unfortunately have nothing to eat. They are hungry and do not know when they will be able to find food again. Think of people living in abject poverty: the homeless, people living in areas ravaged by war, etc. You and I may be fortunate not to be among these people, we have food, and can eat. But do we still complain? Or do we constantly thank God for giving us the food and the appetite to eat it? It's not a right but a privilege and we must always be thankful to God for the privileges He gives us. We are not better or more loved by God than others, everyone is equal before God, so let us always thank God when we eat but also, let us not forget to pray from the heart for those who have nothing.

Before you complain about your spouse, think of someone who is crying out to God for a companion. Appreciate your husband or wife, even if they are not behaving well; change them with your prayers and love if you can.

Today before you complain about life, think of someone who died too young. Before you complain about your children, think of people who desire children but have not been able to have any, through no fault of their own. It is not as if God loves you more than these people, but we know everything God allows to happen, it is for a reason. Appreciate the children God has given you and give them the best training you can. Invest in them physically, materially, emotionally and above all, spiritually. What you deposit in them today, is what they will take into the environment they find themselves in tomorrow. Even when they are not behaving the way you have brought them up to behave, don't give up on then. Continuously carry them in your heart of prayer, nothing is impossible for God.

Before you complain about your house not being as large and attractive as you would like, think of the people living in the streets. There are people who for no fault of their own, have ended up in the streets. Some of these are people who once lived in mansions, but today, they are sleeping rough. So, if you still have roof over your head, just be grateful.

When you are tired and are tempted to complain about your job, think of the unemployed, the disabled, and those who wish they had your job. There are many people who have better qualifications than you, but they can't get a job anywhere because there are unavailable. There are places where it can cost to secure a job you are overqualified for. So, always be grateful for the job you have. If that is where God wants you to be, He can still bless you there. God has promised to make

'A way in the wilderness and streams in the wastelands'

(Isaiah 3:19)

Before you complain about the health care system, where at least you may be getting some things for free, depending on where you come from, have you paused for once to consider that there are so many people who live in areas that receive either very poor health care or none? This may sound strange to you if you have never experienced anything as such. I come from a place where you must pay for every single piece of medical care you receive, from blood tests to x-rays, scans, tablets, etc. Some, after being treated in a hospital, have to stay back until they are able to pay their hospital bills. Some will have to start sleeping in the corridors because they are not allowed to remain in the hospital beds when they have already been discharged. Can you imagine that happening to you?

I remember the day I was involved in a terrible accident and was battling with my life, the doctor of the hospital I was taken to insisted that a huge amount be deposited before he would even touch me to find out what was wrong with me. No amount of pleading from my parents was able to make him change his mind. So, you can imagine what would have happened to me if my parents were not able to rally round and provide the money for the deposit. The same doctor told me a few days after I was admitted that I wouldn't have survived if there hadn't been a quick intervention. This was true, I was having serious internal bleeding because of the accident.

A lot of people have lost their lives because they receive either poor medical care or none. I can remember visiting a renal patient who was receiving dialysis treatment and as we talked, he said to me,

"Do you know, I consider myself very lucky to be receiving this treatment". What he said was no surprise because there are many places where for someone to just have a session of dialysis, huge amounts of money are involved. You can then imagine how many people have died because of kidney failure. This is one of those diseases we refer to as 'big man's disease' because it is only rich men who can afford the treatment and often, they are flown abroad to receive treatment. So as a poor person who has kidney failure, there is no hope, unless there is a miracle. People often resort to self-medication because they can't afford to go to the hospital for treatment. What often happens is they get worse and then have no option other than to go to the hospital. Some may be lucky and recover while others may not make it back alive. Imagine finding yourself in such a situation. Why not be grateful for the health care you are enjoying now, and if it is not good, patiently pray for things to get better.

When depressing thoughts seem to get you down, put a smile on your face and thank God you are alive and still breathing. There are so many things we enjoy and yet take for granted. How many times have you thanked God for the air you breathe – free of charge. I hope you are aware that there are so many people today who are struggling to breathe this same air that we are freely enjoying without any stress. Remember a hungry dog is better than a dead Lion (Ecclesiastes 9:4). Where there is life, there will certainly be hope. Let us ask for the grace to always remain thankful and grateful for all things. The attitude must always be that of gratitude.

Prayer: The Gratitude Prayer

God help us to always look to the many things for which we can be grateful – even amid times of loss.

Let us enjoy the peace that comes with having a grateful heart.

The Bible tells us that it will rain on the just and the unjust, but there is always something to thank you for, God.

Teach us to choose to think about those things so that we may always have a thankful heart.

Amen

Scripture Passages about gratitude:
Ephesians 5:20, 1Thessalonians 5:18, Romans 5:3-5, James 1:1- 4, Colossians 3:1

3

What God Calls You

Most often, we emphasise our limitations more than we do our strengths. We use more of "I can't" than "I can," "I am not" than "I am." We keep focusing on what we don't have rather than what we do have. God knows we have limitations, but He overlooks them and calls us to do things for Him. Remember, God does not call us by our shame; He calls us by our name. He does not call you a weakling, He does not call you an addict, He does not call you a thief, He does not call you anything bad, He calls you His Son or Daughter,

> **'How great is the love the Father has lavished upon us, that we should be called children of God! And that is what we are.'**

> (1 John 3:1)

But the question here is, are we aware that we are His children? The person who does not know who they are will not be who they are meant to be. God Calls us not because we are qualified, but because He wants us. He qualifies us when He calls us. If He were to call us because we are qualified, or because we are good, then none of us would be called, because no one is qualified to be called by God. "Our qualification comes from God alone" (2 Corinthians 3:5).

In Judges 6:12, God called Gideon a mighty man of fearless courage. Now Gideon looked around and said, 'God couldn't be talking about me. I come from the poorest family. I am the least one in my father's house.' Gideon saw himself as weak, defeated, and not able. But God saw him as strong, confident, and more than a conqueror. The question is are we going to believe what God says about us, or are we going to believe what we feel, what we think, or what the circumstances look like? You may feel like a victim, but God Calls you a Victor. You may be afraid, but God Calls you confident. You may be in debt, but God Calls you prosperous. You may be sick, but God Calls You a healthy son or daughter. You may be addicted, but God Calls you free. You may feel inadequate, but God Calls you well-able.

It doesn't matter what people are calling you, what matters is for you to be aware of who God says you are. Just know that the way God sees you is completely different from how people see you, and what God calls you is also different from what people are calling you. Do you know why? This is what Isaiah 55:8 says,

'" For my thoughts are not your thoughts, neither are your ways my ways," declares the LORD.'

There are other passages in the scripture that confirm this too:

'The counsel of the LORD stands forever, the purposes of His heart to all generations.'

(Psalm 33:11)

'The LORD of Hosts has sworn: "As I have planned, so will it be as I have purposed, so will it stand.'

(Isaiah 14:24)

Let us look at the story of the adulterous woman who received forgiveness from Jesus as recorded in John 8:1-11. It is one of the instances of Jesus calling someone, something different from the names that others were calling him or her. William Earnhardt presents the story in a very dramatic way in his write up entitled. *'They Called Her a Whore, Jesus Called Her a Woman.'* This is how he puts it:

'He told her he loved her. Said she was beautiful. Promised her she would be special. Next thing she knew she was being dragged out of bed by the friends of his who had dragged her into bed, and he who had praised and flattered her just stood and watched her being dragged away.

Now she was kneeling half naked, humiliated before Jesus. Eyes

30

closed, not wanting to see the stones that would soon be crushing her head, she waited in terror. It seemed like an eternity. When would it be over?

Barely peeking through one eye she sees Jesus doing something in the sand. Not sure what. She hears footsteps as men walk away. What is going on? Then she hears a word she had not heard in years directed at her.

"Woman...'

Jesus didn't call her a "slut," or "whore." He called her "woman." He was addressing her with the same title of respect that He gave to his own mother, who spoke with angels and gave birth to the Son of God.'

They called her all sorts of derogatory names, but Jesus looked at her and called her "Woman". He restored her dignity once again. He did not call her by her shame; He called her by her name.

This reminds me of the song by the popular American based gospel singer – Sinach, which says 'I know who I am'.

Here are the lyrics from the song:

"I know who God says I am, what he says I am,

Where he says am at, I know who I am,

I know who God says I am, what he says I am,

Where he says am at, I know who I am.

I'm working in power; I walk in miracles.

I live a life of favour, Cos I know who I am"

Another verse of the song says:

"Take a look at me I'm a wonder

It doesn't matter what you see now, can you see his glory.

'cause I know who I am, take a look at me I'm wonder,

It doesn't matter what you see now,

31

Can you see his glory, 'cause I know who I am.

Something we need to know is that if we do not know who we are, or rather, who God calls us, then we will not know where we are meant to be. If you don't know your identity, then you can never know your purpose nor your destination.

You might be wondering at this point, what God calls you. You may be thinking, "What does God say about me? Who does He say that I am?" Let me take you through the scriptures in order to help you with the answers to these important questions.

God says we are valuable. Yes, that means you too. Why does He say so? He is our creator, and we are His creation. He is so in love with us all. He created us in His image. (Genesis 1:27) His eye saw our unformed substance (Psalm 139:13), and He knew us even before we were conceived in our mother's womb. He knows the number of hairs on our head, and before a word is on our tongue, He knows it, (Matthew 10:30; Psalm 139:4) We are fearfully and wonderfully made, (Psalm 139:14). He says we are more valuable than many sparrows, (Matthew 10:31).

God says we are the apple of His eye:

'Keep me as the apple of your eye ide me in the shadow of your wings.'

(Psalm 17:8)

'Keep my commands and you will live; guard my teachings as the apple of your eye.'

(Proverbs 7)

'For this is what the LORD Almighty says: "After the Glorious One has sent me against the nations that have plundered you, for whoever touches you touches the apple of his eye. '

(Zachariah 2:8)

'In a desert land, he found him, in a barren and howling

waste. He shielded him and cared for him; he guarded him as the apple of his eye.'

(Deuteronomy 32:10)

God calls us the light of the world, a city set on a hill (Matthew 5:14). He has called us (2 Peter 1:3). He has chosen us (Revelation 17:14). Through Jesus we are victorious (1 Corinthians 15:57). We have a glorious future (Roman 8:18). We are citizens of heaven (Philippians 3:20). We are ambassadors for His Son (2 Corinthians 5:20).

This day, get into agreement with God. No matter what the circumstances look like, you must dig your heels in and say, 'God, I agree with what you call me. I am free, I am forgiven, I am healed, I am useful, and I can do all things through the strength that comes from you.' Accept what God Calls you and it will make a great difference in your life.

Prayer:

Lord, I pray that You will unlock my heart, that I might be fully alive to my true identity in You. Give me clear revelation to see myself the way You see me. Help me to stand in Your truth against all enemy attacks and guard my heart with all vigilance (Prov 4:23).

Help me to identify the lies and reveal to me any places where I am negatively chained to the past. I repent of any lies of the past. [Name those lies and ask God to forgive you.] Teach me to hear Your voice and not believe the enemy's destructive lies about who I am. I thank You for my uniqueness and that I am made in Your image (Gen 1:27).

I want to understand and feel the deep things in Your heart for me (1 Corinthians 2:10-12).

I choose to believe the truth about how You see me. I thank You that I can hope in the future and believe in the good destiny that You have for me. You have a vision for my future. Help me to live a fruitful life now and overflow with

Your love for others. Give me greater authority in my prayer life. I want to know You on a deeper level, and I don't want anything to hinder my relationship with You.

Debbie Przybylski

4
Do Not Change Your Nature

Sometimes, because of certain experiences we have had in life, we are tempted to change our nature, we behave differently from the way God has made us. I often hear people say:

"I think I will, stop being kind because my kindness is not helping me", or,

"I think I will stop being generous because people don't appreciate my generosity," or,

"I think I will stop being caring because people are always taking my caring nature for granted",

"I think I will stop loving because I have suffered lots of heartbreaks",

and so on and so forth.

The question is, "Is there anything we have at the moment that has not been given to us by God?" Scripture says that every good thing comes from God. Even when we do something good, we are only returning what we have received. We don't qualify for anything of our own accord. Our qualification says St Paul, comes from God. Should we then want to change our good nature because of someone or something?

I would like to share this story with you:

An old man saw a scorpion drowning and decided to pull it out from the water. He calmly put his hand out to reach the creature. When he did, the scorpion stung him. With the effect of the pain, the old man let go of the creature and it fell back into the water. The old man, realising that the scorpion was drowning again, tried to rescue it once more, but again it stung him. He let go of it again.

A young boy standing by approached the old man and said, 'Excuse me Sir are going to hurt yourself trying to save the evil, vicious creature why do you insist? Don't you realise that each time you try to help the scorpion it stings you?'

The man replied,

'The nature of the scorpion is to sting and mine is to help. I will not change my nature in a way that prevents me from helping the scorpion.' So, the man thought for a while and used a leaf from a nearby tree to pull the scorpion out from the water and save its life. Then turning to the little boy, he said, 'Do not change your nature. If someone hurts you, just take precautions. Some pursue happiness while others create it. Let your conscience be your guide in whatever you do. When life presents you with a hundred reasons to be angry, show it that you have a thousand and more reasons to smile. More importantly, always be the reason for that precious smile on someone else's face.'

During our lives we are bound to experience hurts, disappointments, heartbreaks, and the like, even when we try to please people. I understand that because of our human nature, there will always be a time when we will want to say enough is enough. No one wants to continue being hurt. But as the man in the story said, we cannot just give up on being who we are simply because of the bad behaviour of others. I know it is easier said than done. It can appear difficult or even impossible for us, but when we involve God, then it becomes possible. St Paul says,

'I can do all things through Christ who strengthens me.'

(Philippians 4:13)

When we involve God, we will no longer say that we have had enough and can't continue this way anymore, instead, we can take a tougher approach and show that people's bad nature can never make us change our own nature, even though we have been hurt on several occasions. Refuse to change, if whatever you are doing is for the sake of God.

Imagine Jesus himself, He is our perfect example. Consider what He went through, even after showing such great love and mercy, along with performing amazing signs and wonders, He was treated with rejection, mockery, ridicule, accusations, hatred, brutality and extreme torture. Notwithstanding all these things, He never gave up, He chose to bear all of it and more for our sake, out of the immeasurable love He has for us. We too, should try to bear our burden out of our love for God.

Are you thinking of changing your nature? The only part of our nature that is meant to be changed is the negative part, especially when it affects our relationship with God and our fellow human beings. There is something good in you that God wants you to use for the service of others. Don't let anyone change your good nature. Don't let bitter, unhappy people drag you down to their level. Instead, use their behaviour as an example of how not to behave and be grateful you are nothing like them. Proverbs 3:27 says:

'Do all you can for everyone who deserves your help. Withhold not good from them to whom it is due, when it is in the power of thy hand to do it. Do not withhold him from doing good, who is able. If you are able, do good yourself.'

So, is there someone you used to help before, but have stopped because the person was not appreciating you? Have a re-think. Don't allow that person to take from you the grace of goodness that God has given you. Keep doing the good you know how to do. Don't change your nature. Your reward awaits you.

'... He is a rewarder of them that diligently seek him.'

(Hebrews 11:6)

Prayer:
Heavenly Father, thank you for making me the way I am. Help me to appreciate your grace working in me. May I never try to change whatever good you have put into me because of the bad attitude of others. Let me always appreciate and cherish the good that is in me while making a great effort to

change the bad in me, trusting in your power to transform me for the better. Then Father, please use me as you desire. *Amen.*

5

When You Think all Hope is Lost

Have you ever felt that nothing could be done about a particular situation you found yourself in at any point in your life? I believe that all of us at one point or another have had these unwelcome experiences. If it happens that you have had such an experience, I believe you didn't just go through it, but rather grew through it. To this, Eleanor Roosevelt said, *'You gain strength, courage, and confidence by every experience in which you really stop to look fear in the face. You are able to say to yourself, I lived through this horror. I can take the next thing that comes along.'*

Jesus cares about us always, but especially when problems make us feel hopeless or sad or when we are set aside because of illness. I want to illustrate this fact with the story of the healing of the paralysed man as recorded in John 5: 1-9. See how Jesus reaches out to the man in the story who is at such a low ebb.

> *'Sometime later, Jesus went up to Jerusalem for one of the Jewish festivals. Now there is in Jerusalem near the Sheep Gate a pool, which in Aramaic is called Bethesda and which is surrounded by five covered colonnades. Here a great number of disabled people used to lie – the blind, the lame, the paralyzed. One who was there had been an invalid for thirty-eight years. When Jesus saw him lying there and learned that he had been in this condition for a long time, he asked him, "Do you want to get well?" "Sir," the invalid replied, "I have no one to help me into the pool when the water is stirred. While I am trying to get in, someone else goes down ahead of me." Then Jesus said to him, "Get up! Pick up your mat and walk." At once the man was cured; he picked up his mat and walked.'*

Let us unpack this Gospel story a little. The pool at Bethesda was thought to have healing powers. The belief was that whenever the pool stirred or troubled, the first person who managed to enter it would be healed. One of the men waiting at the pool was in a hopeless state. He was unable to walk and that had been his condition for 38 years. There could be a few reasons why he was unable to walk, but certainly after all those years his legs were withered and totally useless. This man had been brought to the pool, but he knew that he could never get into the water in time if indeed the water stirred. What we are interested in here is Jesus' encounter with this man.

Jesus met him lying close to the pool. Now, when Jesus asked him if he wanted to be healed, his answer was not Yes or No, but,

'I have no one to help me into the pool when the water is stirred. While I am trying to get in, someone else goes down ahead of me.'

Notice from his response, that he had been going to the pool regularly since he became ill, and yet, not a single person had offered to help him. I guess they were all busy with their own problems, too busy to notice him.

Sometimes we are also too busy with ourselves so that we don't notice others around us who may need our help. We can imagine the man's frustration from the answer he gave to Jesus, but I think this man still has something else to teach us. He had been coming to the pool persistently for almost 38 years and yet no one had offered to help him to get into the pool. Let me emphasise, it was not as though the man had been going to Bethesda for 38 days or 38 months, but for 38 long years. He had continued going there even though he knew it was unlikely that anyone would help him into the pool. Clearly, he was not ready to give up, even when things seemed hopeless for Him. As Christians, are we able to wait on God that long? Can we still trust Him when it looks like the future is bleak? Do we really think God is worth waiting for?

After 38 years, this man's problem had become a way of life. No one had ever helped him. He had no hope of ever being healed. His situation looked completely hopeless. Who knows, he may have been mocked or laughed at by some people every time he was unable to jump into the pool like the others. Imagine the heartbreak, frustration and depression he would have gone through, but, when Jesus entered the scene, He noticed him straight away.

> **'When Jesus saw him lying there and learned that he had been in this condition for a long time, he asked him, "Do you want to get well?"'**

(John 5:6)

In Isaiah 49:8, the word of God says,

> **'Thus says the Lord: At the time of my favour, I have answered you, on the day of salvation I have helped you.'**

God has his appointed or favoured time. No matter how long it takes, He is never late but arrives at the right time. For us it may seem to have taken ages, but we must understand that He is not limited to time. He often comes when we are not expecting Him. See how He reached out to help the poor man even though he hadn't called out for His help at that time, but we don't know how many prayers he had sent up to God for so many years, – perhaps desperate prayers, knowing that God's help was his only hope. Then when the time was right, Jesus Himself came to his aid. When we are feeling hopeless, He comes and brings us restoration. No matter how trapped you feel by your problems, God can minister to your deepest needs. Don't let a problem or hardship cause you to lose hope. Don't give up too soon, because you know what? Giving up is never an option.

Prayer:

Emmanuel, Lord God Almighty, I praise Your holy name. Today, Lord, I feel so tired, weary and discouraged. The only way I see out of this is to give up totally.

41

Things seem ever so gloomy. Nothing is going my way. Although I still have some hope that this situation is going to turn around, the little that I have fades into the shadows, daily.

I welcome the Presence of the Holy Spirit. Let Him be my Comforter and Guide. I acknowledge that I may need to make difficult changes in my life. But, making changes isn't giving up, doing nothing when I need to, is.

I know that my present struggles do not mean I am a failure because every great success requires some kind of struggle to get there.

Father, illness, my relationships, and my job, are all getting the better of me. Give me strength. Give me hope. As I cling to You, please draw near.

Uplift my Spirit, oh Lord. Give me peace, give me joy. Give me happiness. I need hope. You alone can turn this around, for You are magnificent, wonderful, and powerful and will never leave me or forsake me.

I am your child and whatever I ask for, I surely will receive. Worry ends where faith begins, and I trust that You, Oh God, will lead me to victory.

Be with me every day. As victory approaches the throne of grace, mercy, suffering, discouragement, doubt and despair will surely leave my mind today. In JESUS' mighty name, *Amen.*

Scripture passages to remember in times of need: *Here are 10 bible verses to remember for when you need a reminder that there is still hope:*

Jeremiah 29:11, John 13:7, 1 Peter. 5:10, Exodus 14:13-14, Deuteronomy 31:6, Deuteronomy 31:8, Romans 8:18, 2 Kings. 20:5.

6
Appreciate The Good in Others

'And Joshua the son of Nun, the minister of Moses, one of his chosen men, said, "My Lord Moses, forbid them." But Moses said to him, "Are you Jealous for my sake? Would that the entire Lord's people were prophets, that the Lord would put his spirit upon them!"'

(Numbers 11:28-29)

'But Jesus said, "Do not forbid him; for no one who does mighty work in my name will be able soon afterward to speak evil of me."'

(Mark 9:39)

If we are honest with ourselves, we realize that there are times when, we are not too comfortable with other people's good progress and development, especially when we think we should be better. This results in jealousy and anger. This is exactly what we see in the gospel reading in Mark 9:38-43, 47-48. The disciples, prior to that time were unable to cast out the demon in a young boy that was brought to them. As we see in Mark 9:18, It was not long after that incident that they saw another man doing exactly what they were commissioned to do but had failed to do in the case of the demoniac boy. Therefore, they became jealous of the man, got angry with him and tried to stop him.

John, as we saw in the gospel, was delegated by the apostles to report the incident to Jesus as his beloved disciple, but Jesus used the opportunity to teach them a very important lesson about the gifts of God. The gift of God is like wind that blows wherever it wills. It is like a kite that lands wherever the wind takes it. God is open with his gifts to those who sincerely need them and are willing to work with them. Even when human constraints limit what we can achieve, God is there to intervene because all he wants is for his will to be done. That is why even though the other man had not been chosen as a disciple, Jesus still allowed him to possess and make use of the gift of healing in his name. All we need to do is to have the right intention.

The feeling of Jealousy arises when we fail to see the gift of God in our lives or when we are not content with whatever gift we have. It is like a parent giving different gifts of the same value to two siblings, one of them may become upset and jealous because he or she feels that the other's is better than theirs. Even though God gives everyone different gifts, each gift He has given to is special, and it is these gifts that make us unique. So, when I recognize this fact, I should cherish my gift as special, make good use of it, and then it will surely make way for me. Proverbs 18:16 says,

'A man's gift makes room for him and brings him before great men.' (NKJV)

For us to appreciate the good in others, we must first and foremost recognize our own gifts and appreciate them. The fact is, what we can't appreciate in ourselves, we can't appreciate in others. What we can't see in ourselves, we can't see in others. If I know that there is something special God has given to me, then I shouldn't become jealous when I see something special about another person.

I really love what Kim Thompson-Pinder wrote about this in his article, *'Your gift will make room for you – Proverbs 18:16 Explained'* published at *Faithisland.org*. He writes:

'One of the first things you need to understand is that God has given you gifts to use for His glory. Yes, You! You may be thinking to yourself, 'I am not important enough for God to give me a gift,

skill, or a talent.' God created you for the purpose of His Kingdom going forward. He has enabled you to reach people that no one else can, and it is the gifts He has given to you that accomplish it. Romans 12:6 says,

> **'having then gifts differing according to the grace that is given to us, let us use them**.'

Second, you need to understand that your gifts are unique to you. Don't look at what someone else can do and wish that was you. You may think your talent is weird and unpopular, but sometimes it is those of us who feel like we have the least to give who accomplish great things for God. Look at Gideon. (Judges 6) Everyone judged him and thought he was a coward because he hid away in a winepress to thresh wheat in safety. You know what God saw? Someone who would not give up and would think outside of the box to survive and defy the enemy. The enemy of our souls wants to make you feel like your gift is useless and that there is no way your gift can make a difference. Your gift does make a difference.'

When we come to a full understanding and realisation of God's gifts in our lives, it helps us to appreciate the gifts in the lives of others. So, instead of getting jealous over other people's gifts, we will appreciate and give thanks for what they have, knowing that there is something they have that we don't, and there is something we have, that they don't have.

Jesus' response in the gospel passage we looked at earlier confirms the position of Moses as regards the gifts of God as we saw in Numbers 11:16-17, 25-29. Let us take a further look at that passage of scripture,

> **'So, Moses went out and told the people what the LORD had said. He brought together seventy of their elders and had them stand around the tent. Then the LORD came down in the cloud**

and spoke with him, and he took some of the power of the Spirit that was on him and put it on the seventy elders. When the Spirit rested on them, they prophesied but did not do so again. However, two men, whose names were Eldad and Medad, had remained in the camp. They were listed among the elders but did not go out to the tent. Yet the Spirit also rested on them, and they prophesied in the camp. A young man ran and told Moses, "Eldad and Medad are prophesying in the camp." Joshua son of Nun, who had been Moses' aide since youth, spoke up and said, "Moses, my LORD, stop them!" But Moses replied, "Are you jealous for my sake? I wish that all the LORD's people were prophets and that the LORD would put his Spirit on them!"'

Seventy men were prepared to receive the spirit of Moses, but human constraints prevented two men from appearing at the tent, yet they received the Spirit and also prophesied to the jealousy and anger of other Israelites, especially Joshua.

This is meant to teach us something great about God. God's ways are not our ways and He is infinite in all perfections. This is why we should not try to limit or predict what God can do. He can raise up anybody anywhere to do for him those things that maybe, because of feelings of Jealousy or envy, we have refused to do for Him. He is free to bless even when we feel less favoured because all works are to the glory of God. We become jealous of the good of others when we work for our own glory and not for the glory of God. But working for the glory of God, will enable us to appreciate and encourage the good we see in others. If you have a particular talent and discover that another person has the same talent, be appreciative to God for that, then encourage that person to be the best he or she can be by making good use of their talent, but do not try to stop them, or pull them down, (P.H.D syndrome, meaning, Pull him/her Down because of jealousy). But do not be afraid when you think you fall outside the line, God can still use you if you are prepared.

Furthermore, we should also remember that the good gifts we have, be them material or spiritual, are for the good of those around us, including those who are annoyed with us for possessing them. We should not use them to intimidate or humiliate others but instead use them to build up the people of God. That is why St James warns the rich to be careful of the paths they tread especially against the poor, (James 5:1-6).

Finally, let us always be aware that God has blessed all of us in one way or another. Let us always appreciate whatever God has given to us and be content with it. Every gift God has given to us is good and valuable in His sight. We must therefore learn to value it in our lives and the lives of others.

Scripture passages about appreciating the good in others:
1 Thessalonians 5:18, James 1:17, 1 Timothy 4:4.

Prayer:

Thank you, Lord, for the blessings you have bestowed upon my life. You have provided me with more than I could ever have imagined. You have surrounded me with people who always look out for me. You have given me family and friends who bless me every day with kind words and actions. They lift me up in ways that keep my eyes focused on you and make my spirit soar.

Also, thank you, Lord, for keeping me safe. You protect me from those things that seem to haunt others. You help me make better choices, and you have provided me with advisors that help me with difficult decisions. You speak to me in so many ways that I always know you are here.

And Lord, I am so grateful to you for keeping those around me safe and loved. I hope that you provide me with the ability and sense to show them every day how much they matter. I hope that you give me the ability to give to them the same kindness they have provided to me. I am just so grateful for all your blessings in my life. Lord, I pray that you remind me of just how lucky I am, and that you never allow me to forget to show my gratitude in prayer and return kind acts. Thank you, Lord. In your name,

Amen.

Kelli Mahoney

7
Arise, Don't Stay Down!

I recall an incident that took place in my secondary school days. There was one particular year when we had our 'inter-house sport competitions'. Students were normally grouped into houses and then they competed among themselves. Each house had at least one representative in different sport competitions. In the 200 metres race there was no one to represent my house, so at the last minute, I decided to do it myself. Others had practised and knew what was required in this race.

If you are not fully prepared for the event you must set off slowly because in this race you must run round the football field twice to finish. So, if you don't take it easy, you will tire very quickly and may end up not finishing the race. Because I had not practised and was ignorant of the tactics required for the race, I zoomed off at high speed as soon as I heard the whistle and was running ahead of the others. I was wondering why they were not running as fast as I was. Until halfway I kept up the pace, but then, I found that my energy was almost gone. Not only that, but I was also losing my breath. I was struggling, but then with the cheers from my house members, "Go Alvan, Go Alvan," I tried to keep moving but was now well behind all the others. I felt like I was going to pass out, but I didn't want people to laugh at me ... yet also, in conflict with this rushing through my mind was the thought that collapsing altogether would be even worse! So, I fell and lay in a heap on the field. Then came a voice: "Alvan, you can't remain there, arise and finish up at least". Immediately, I heard that voice, which I believe was our house master's, my strength returned, I jumped up and started running again and never stopped till I got to the end. By then I had been able to pass a few people at least. I didn't come first, second or third, but the most important thing was I did finish the race. I didn't give up even when I fell, I arose and continued. My target was to finish the race and I did. It didn't matter what position I achieved at the end of the race, what mattered was that I finished it.

In our lives, we see ourselves falling in different ways. We may have fallen at our academic stage, in our business, in our job, in our love life, in our spiritual life, in our family life, etc. But listen to this if you fall it does not make you a failure. You become a failure only when you have accepted that you are one. According to Joel Osteen,

'When you get knocked down, don't stay down, get back up again. Nothing good is going to happen as long as you are down yourself' and according to Mohammed Ali, *'You don't lose if you get knocked down; you lose if you stay down.'*

So even when you fall, which will often happen, don't just stay down, you can still rise and keep going. With determination, you can always finish the race. Remember, the downfall of a person is not the end of his or her life, it does not matter how many times you have fallen you can always stand up again. Israelmore Ayivor in his work, *'The Great Handbook of Quotes'*, has this to say,

'Leave no 'full stop' between the sentences that make up your life story. If anything, let 'commas' show that when you were brought down by challenges, you rose up with passion and moved on again.'

Don't mind if people are laughing at you and teasing you, your destiny belongs not to them, or to any man but to God, who lifts the fallen. Here is what the prophet Micah has to say,

'Do not gloat over me, my enemy! Though I have fallen, I will rise. Though I sit in darkness, the Lord will be my light.'

(Micah 7:8)

My beloved, have you fallen? Then you must not remain on the ground. You must stand up and continue. Remember God says He is going to bring you to your expected end. But you must stand up and keep moving till you reach the end. It doesn't matter how long it may take, with determination, resoluteness, and absolute trust in

God for strength, you will certainly reach your destination at the appointed time.

We may find that there are things in our lives that get in the way of our relationship with God, perhaps it is circumstances, situations, or certain people. The good news is, God is always ready to help you. You must break free, do not let anyone or anything stop you from reaching out to the Master. You don't need to sit back in anguish, depression, or self-pity. In faith, reach out to the Master, and you will never be the same again. No one who encountered Jesus remained the same. But it is very important, that you remain unstoppable.

In Luke 8:42-48 we find the story of Jesus healing the woman with the issue of blood. We are told that she had endured the problem for 12 long years. She had spent all her money on doctors to tend her, but no one had been able to cure her. Maybe she used to be very rich, who knows? but now she practically has nothing. I believe she used to have a lot of friends, but at this point, they have all disappeared and abandoned her. We will often only discover our true friends when problems arise, as unfortunately, that is the time when many so-called 'friends' disappear!

There was a Lady in my former parish who had multiple sclerosis and I used to visit her when her condition deteriorated, and she couldn't come to church anymore. One day I asked her if she still had her friends come and visit her because I knew she used to be so popular in the parish. She told me, with tears in her eyes,

"Father, do you know, almost all my close friends have left me. Some even call me on the phone to say they can't continue being my friend because they don't feel they can help me anymore. It is heart-breaking for me as those I need at this point have all abandoned me. I never expected this, yet I don't feel too bad about it because my family has been good to me, and I know God has not left Me."

It was sad to hear that from this lady who has now died. God rest her soul. Sadly, this is often how it is in life, and I imagine it was also the experience the woman with the issue of blood had. But there is one friend we can be sure will always be there for us, in good times and in bad. He is Jesus. Even when everyone has given up on you, He will never give up on you. So don't you give up, – be strong in faith. Jesus will never abandon you.

Just imagine what this woman was going through. She represents many of us. She was a person who was familiar with intense physical and emotional pain as well as financial distress. She was someone under severe pressure, who was rejected by society because of her condition. Of course, nobody would want to go around with a person who would smell so terribly because of the constant flow of blood from her body. Imagine how it would feel to be losing blood every day for 12 years. Apart from the terrible inconvenience, smell, and rejection, she must have felt very unwell, weak, and exhausted.

Amidst all these things, she had a choice. She must have heard about the Master, who was going about doing good. She made up her mind to touch Him when she saw Him coming amid the crowd. Remember, she could have stayed in her house crying all day long and abusing God for imposing such suffering upon her. She could have chosen to do away with anything about Jesus and His so-called teaching. Had she done so, she would have missed her opportunity to encounter Him and would have been accepting the conclusions of the doctors and people who must have told her that her condition was hopeless. But hear this, 'No condition before God is hopeless. She made up her mind, she said to herself,

'If I only touch his cloak, I will be healed.'

(Mat 9:21)

She didn't care what anyone thought. She didn't care about what people would say. She was not interested in how people would react. No doubt, these things all came to her mind to discourage her, but she didn't allow them to stop her. She had one goal, and that was to touch the hem of Jesus' garment. She pressed forward and kept on going regardless of the opposition and obstacles in her way until finally, she touched Jesus.

'Make a commitment to yourself that today, success is your only option. No matter the obstacles, no matter the sacrifice! You have decided you won't be denied you won't be defeated.'

(Eric Thomas)

Immediately she touched Jesus, the incurable problem she had endured for 12 years disappeared. The problem that no earthly doctor could heal, was no match for Jesus. Matt 9:22 says,

'And the woman was healed from that moment.'

But remember it was all because of the unstoppable faith of this woman that this happened. When Jesus saw her, he said,

'Your faith has healed you.'

Beloved, do not be stopped from going to Jesus, the friend who loves you so much. It does not matter how long you have pushed. There is never a time to give up because of things or people. Keep pushing, the Master is waiting for you to touch Him with your faith like that woman. Just say to yourself, 'By the power of His grace working in me, I will remain unstoppable by the situations that form around me.' God bless you with His grace, Amen.

Prayer:
Lord, You are the wind in my sails.
You guide me as I steer and find direction.
You give me the strength to keep on going.
You watch over me as I navigate stormy seas.
You are the harbour where I stop for rest.
You are my encourager when I lose hope.
You are the lighthouse that keeps my path safe.
You are with me always.
Thank you.
Amen.

(a short prayer of encouragement from www.Lords-prayer-words.com)

8
He Hears Our Cries!

Today, a lot of people have given up on God because they feel that He does not hear the cries and groans of His people. This may be because of experiences they have had in which they continually prayed for God's intervention, and when they didn't get the answers they wanted, concluded that God must be deaf and insensitive to the cries of His people. That is the point where they decided they were done with God. I have also been in a situation when I cried out to God and He did not answer in the way I wanted, or as quickly as I wanted. But I didn't give up on God and He certainly didn't give up on me. I will share my own experience later in this chapter.

The big question we need to ask here is: does God hear the cry of His people? Is He just like one of those other gods who have eyes but can't see people's tears, who have ears but can't hear people's cries and feel people's pain?

Well, let us look at some passages from the scriptures. Maybe they will give us a clue as to the answer to this question. I strongly believe that the God of the scriptures is still the God of today who never changes, for He says in Malachi 3:6,

"I am the Lord, I changeth not."

If the God of the scriptures heard the voice of His people when they cried out, and if He is still the same God, we call on today, then that means He still hears our cries. Let us now look at these few passages from the scripture:

'The LORD hears those who cry out, and he delivers them from all their distress.'

Psalm4:17)

'Now it came about in the course of those many days that the king of Egypt died. And the sons of Israel sighed

because of the bondage, and they cried out; and their cry for help because of their bondage rose up to God'

(Exodus 2:23)

'As Pharaoh drew near, the sons of Israel looked, and behold, the Egyptians were marching after them, and they became very frightened; so, the sons of Israel cried out to the LORD.'

(Exodus 14:10)

'Moses cried out to the LORD, saying, "What shall I do to these people? A little more and they will stone me."'

(Exodus 17:4)

'When the sons of Israel cried to the LORD, the LORD raised up a deliverer for the sons of Israel to deliver them, Othniel the son of Kenaz, Caleb's younger brother.'

(Judges 3:9)

'As Pharaoh approached, the Israelites looked up and saw the Egyptians marching after them, and they were terrified and cried out to the LORD.'

(Exodus 14:10)

Did the Lord hear their voice when they cried out to Him? Yes, He did, and He delivered them from the captivity of the Egyptians. The next passage from Deuteronomy is a testimony to this.

'For what nation is so great as to have a god as near to them as the LORD our God is to us whenever we call on Him?'

(Deuteronomy 4:7)

They themselves testified that God always heard them whenever they cried out to Him.

'And the LORD said to him, "I have heard your prayer and petition before Me. I have consecrated this temple you have built by putting My Name there forever; My eyes and My heart will be there for all time."'

(1 Kings 9:3)

This was an answer to the prayers and supplications made by King Solomon in 1 Kings 8 to dedicate the temple he built for the Lord. His prayer was answered as recorded in chapter 9.

'They were helped against them, and the Hagrites and all who were with them were given into their hand; for they cried out to God in the battle, and He answered their prayers because they trusted in Him.'

(1Chronicles 5:20)

'When Judah turned around, behold, they were attacked both front and rear; so, they cried to the LORD, and the priests blew the trumpets.'

(2 Chronicles 13:14)

'Hear, O our God, how we are despised! Return their reproaches on their own heads and give them up for plunder in a land of captivity.'

(Nehemiah 4:4)

'Then Asa called to the LORD his God and said, "LORD, there is no one besides You to help in the battle between the powerful and those who have no strength; so, help us, O LORD our God, for we trust in You, and in Your name have come against this multitude. O LORD, You are our God; let not man prevail against you."'

(2 Chronicles 14:11)

'This poor man called out, and the LORD heard him; He saved him from all his troubles.'

(Psalm 34:6)

'He fulfils the desires of those who fear Him; He hears their cry and saves them.'

(Psalm 145:19)

'He shall call upon me, and I will answer him: I *will be* with him in trouble; I will deliver him and honour him.'

(Psalm 91:15)

'The LORD *is* nigh unto all them that call upon him, to all that call upon him in truth.'

(Psalm 145:18-20)

Apart from the Israelites who were constantly crying out to the Lord in their distress, the Bible is full of examples of times when God answered the cries of His people. Below are a few examples of occasions on which individuals cried out to God and God heard their cries and delivered them:

- Elijah cried out, and God revived a dead child. (I Kings 17:20–22)
- Jehoshaphat cried out, and God delivered him from death. (II Chronicles 18:31)
- Hezekiah cried out, and God gave him victory. (II Chronicles 32:20–21)
- Hannah cried out, and God answered her and gave her Samuel. (1 Samuel 1:1-20)
- Jabez cried out, and God granted his request and changed his fortune. (1 Chronicles 4:10)
- Shadrach, Meshach and Abednego cried out, and God delivered them from the burning furnace. (Daniel 3: 1-30)
- Daniel cried out, and God delivered him from the Lion's den. (Daniel 6:1-28)
- Jesus' disciples cried out to Him in a storm, and Jesus calmed the sea. (Luke 8:23–24).
- Blind Bartimaeus called to Jesus, and He restored his sight. (Mark 10:46)

Even in our own time, there are so many people who will testify that God still hears the cries of His people, not because of what they have read in the scriptures but because of what He has done in their lives. Proudly, with conviction, I can say that I am one of those people. Countless times I have cried out to Him in distress, and He has listened to the voice of my cry. Several times when all hope seemed lost, I called out to Him and He answered. When I was almost about to lose my right arm because of the carelessness of the doctors involved in the treatment, I cried out to Him and He saved me. Several times when I got myself into trouble, I cried out to Him, He saved me and gave me another chance.

He also answered the cries of my family. On many occasions, the enemy came with full force to attack and bring shame to our family, but we cried out to Him and He speedily came to our rescue. Some years ago, my dad became seriously sick in a way we had never seen before. I took him to different hospitals and various diagnoses were made, and treatments were given, yet he kept going downhill every day. He lost so much weight and couldn't even stand for a long period. I believe people must have said a lot of things about his condition. But we cried to the '**God of all possibilities'** (Jeremiah 32:27), for whom nothing is impossible. He answered our cries. My dad whom we thought we had almost lost is still alive today. Dear Friend, God hears the cries of His people, and He will hear you in your time of need.

According to an article, *'What does it mean to cry to God,'* adapted from materials in the *'Anger Resolution seminar':* *'Crying out to God is an act of desperation and total concentration. It is a fervent expression of faith in God and trust in His goodness and power to act on your behalf.'* It went on to say that crying to God expresses the following traits:

'**Genuine humility'** (Psalm 9:12); '**absolute surrender'** (Psalm 66:18); '**a plea for mercy'** (Lamentation 3:22-23); '**personal helplessness'** (John 15:5); '**faith in God's power and resources'** (Matthew 8:25) and '**desperation'** (Psalm 18:6)

Imagine a nursing mother hearing the voice of her crying child. She would rush to attend to her baby. Everything else would have to wait until she had seen to the needs of her little one. Remember you are God's little one.

The scripture says in the book of Isaiah 30:19,

> **'He will surely be gracious to you at the sound of your cry; when He hears it, He will answer you.'**

This promise to the suffering Israelites recalls God's faithfulness in answering the prayers of His people when they cried out to Him for help. In situations of our own, we too can cry out to God, asking Him to come near, to guide us and teach us. (Is 30:20-21).

We must believe that God does hear our prayers when we cry to him for help. Think of the New Testament promises:

'Ask and it will be given to you.'

(Lk 11:9)

Recall the words of Matthew's gospel:

> **'When He (Jesus) saw the crowds, He had compassion for them, because they were harassed and helpless, like sheep without a shepherd.'**

(Mt 9:30)

Even when we are confused or troubled to the point of not knowing what or how to pray, we can be certain that the Holy Spirit within us knows what we need better than we do, and that He will cry out with us to our loving Father. (Rom 8:26,27)

Grace Houle writes,

'When we express the desires of our heart in prayer, they don't fall on deaf ears. Yet sometimes when we don't get a quick response, or exactly what we desire, we huff and puff and say God isn't listening. God sees the full picture even when we only see a small piece of the puzzle. We just have to keep the faith that God knows what's best. Don't be discouraged if you don't get an

answer right away. Keep on asking until God answers, and when He does, pray that God prepares your heart so you can accept the outcome.'

One thing we need to know is that God always hears our cries in prayer. It doesn't matter how long it may take, what matters is the voice of prayer must never be silent. So, don't give up crying to Him because your senses are telling you that He is not hearing your voice. As you may already know, God answers prayers in three different ways. He can say "Yes," "No," or "wait a bit." In all these ways be sure He has answered your prayers, He listened to your cry. But as Grace Houle states, *'When he answers you, pray that God prepares your heart so you can accept the outcome.'* This is all about having the right attitude to accept God's will for us.

To some of our prayers, God says "Yes." Sometimes, He says yes so that by seeing what He has done for us, others will come to believe in Him. If the time is right, and we are asking for something that we need, and if He knows it is something that will be good for us, then He will always say, "Yes". He may use His answer to draw us closer to Him. The scripture records in 1 Chronicles 4:9-10 a man named Jabez-

> **'Jabez was more honourable than his brother. His mother had named him Jabez, saying, "I gave birth to him in pain." Jabez cried out to the God of Israel, "Oh that you would bless me and enlarge my territory! Let your hand be with me and keep me from harm so that I will be free from pain." And God granted his request**.'

To some of our prayers, God can say "wait." Often it may be that what we are asking for is good for us, but the timing is not. God's ways are different from ours, so also is His timing. He always has an appointed time and when that time comes, He will surely say "yes," if not, His answer will be for us to wait until the right time. He may also say wait when He wants us to learn something from a particular circumstance. We may be impatient, and He may want to teach us how to be patient by delaying the answer to our prayers. He may still want to teach us something else, and for us to learn the lesson, we must wait patiently for Him. When we have learned that lesson, God's answer will then be, "Yes," if it is in accordance with His will. It is all about being patient.

In 2004 I had a bad accident and stayed out of school because of it. I had a fractured arm, and because of it, I couldn't write, so, it would have been difficult to stay in school. I did try but I felt I was a burden for my lovely roommate who had to bring my food from the refectory every day and wash my clothes.

After a while, I decided to go back home and stay there until my fractured arm healed completely. I prayed and cried to God every night to heal my hand so that I could go back and join my classmates. Funnily enough, my main problem was not just for my bone to heal, but rather that I didn't want to be left behind by my classmates. I just wanted everything to happen so fast, but God was saying to me, "Wait! Wait!! Wait!" I just didn't want to hear that. The only answer I wanted to my prayers was, "Yes."

Lisa Jones once said,

'If 'Yes' is the answer we most want to hear and 'no' is the answer that most disappoints, 'not now' must be most frustrating. It is neither Yes nor No and requires something more: patience."

God was saying to me, "Wait, not now." This was because he had something He was preparing for me that I never knew about. I said to Him, 'Ok Lord, I am no longer in a hurry. I have seen you want me to be not ahead of you but behind you so that you will lead me through all this. Now let your will be done. I surrender everything into your hands'. It was only when I calmed down that I learnt the lesson God was teaching me, and things began falling into place again. It was Job in the bible who said,

'I know the way the Lord is taking me, when He is through, I shall come out as gold.'

God can also say an outright "No" to our request. It is not as if He can't give us what we want, but do we need it, and would it be good for us? God loves us so much and knows what is best for us more than we do. His will for us is perfect. But most often when we pray, we want to force Him into doing our own will. When He says no, what is our reaction? How do we react to God and His church, when we pray and don't receive what we prayed for? Do we feel like giving up on Him and cursing Him? This may be the most difficult answer we get from God, but the fact is that He still answers prayers.

'God may not always answer the prayers we want, but He always answers the prayers we need'

(www.pictureQuotes.com)

When God doesn't answer your prayer, it means He has another plan for you. Just be patient. David shows us what our attitude should be like when this happens. The child that David had illicitly with Bathsheba, fell very sick. David prayed for his healing. He fasted and prayed for his child for 7 days. Yet God didn't heal the baby. After the child's death, David instead of becoming angry with God went into the house of the Lord and worshiped God. To come to the place of realisation that God doesn't always answer our prayers the way we desire is a beautiful thing. God is deserving of our praise, whether He says "Yes" to our request.

Bill Hybels writes,

'If the request is wrong, God says 'No.' If the request is wrong, God says 'slow.' If you are wrong, God says 'grow.' But if the request is right and the timing is right and you are right, God says, 'Yes, Go,'

Let us always be mindful that God will never answer "Yes," to any request that goes against His word.

Until God answers, continue praying, continue crying out. St James in his letter says,

'The effectual fervent prayer of the righteous man availeth much'

(James 5:16)

Pray to the God who hears and can do something about it. But when God answers, we should be willing to accept His response, and be thankful even if it isn't to our heart's desire because God's ways are higher than our ways, and there is a purpose and a plan for His response even if we don't see it right away."

Finally, know this, that when God answers our prayer, He is increasing our faith. If he delays, He is increasing our patience. If He doesn't answer our prayer, He is preparing the best for us. Shalom.

Prayer:
'Shout for joy to God, all the earth! Sing the glory of his name; make his praise glorious. Say to God, "How awesome are your deeds! So great is your power that your enemies cringe before you. All the earth bows down to you, they sing praise to you, they sing the praises of your name. Come and see what God has done, his awesome deeds for mankind! He turned the sea into dry land, they passed through the waters on foot— come, let us rejoice in him. He rules forever by his power, his eyes watch the nations— let not the rebellious revolt against him. Praise our God, all peoples, let the sound of his praise be heard; he has preserved our lives and kept our feet from slipping. For you, God tested us; you refined us like silver. You brought us into prison and laid burdens on our backs. You let people ride over our heads; we went through fire and water, but you brought us to a place of abundance. I will come to your temple with burnt offerings and fulfil my vows to you those vows my lips promised and my mouth spoke when I was in trouble. I will sacrifice fat animals to you and offer rams; I will offer bulls and goats. Come and hear, all you who fear God; let me tell you what he has done for me. I cried out to him with my mouth; his praise was on my tongue. If I had cherished sin in my heart, the Lord would not have listened; but God has surely listened and has heard my prayer. Praise be to God, who has not rejected my prayer or withheld his love from me.'

Psalm 66 (NIV)

9
Don't Let Fear Stop You!

There is no doubt that as human beings we all have our fears. This, I say, is because of the uncertainties in life. No one is certain about what life has in store because life is full of mysteries. This feeling of uncertainty doesn't mean there is anything seriously wrong, but if our fears prevent us from doing the things that we truly want to do, then we have a real problem. Of course, the more the important areas of our lives are affected, the more of a problem we have. Becoming victims of our fears will mean living our fears instead of our dreams. Someone once said,

'Fear has the power to hold you back from taking risks, following your dreams, or becoming successful at anything you wish to do. If you allow it to control you long enough, it can eventually erode your quality of life and keep you locked in a prison of inactivity.'

I think this is very true. In my own life I am aware that fear has held me back from doing a lot of things I should ordinarily have done with ease. But by God's grace I have learned to face my fears. With God's help we don't have to be victims of fear.

I see fear as a veil covering the eyes of the person, preventing him or her from seeing things as they really are and from seeing themselves as they really are. Fear is that feeling that always makes you want to sit down and remain where you are. We all know that if we want to achieve anything in life, we must be ready to stand up and make a move. I now know that this was the reason why I didn't want to stand up in class to answer or ask a question, even when I knew the answer or what to ask. It was fear keeping me down, fear that I may not have the right answer, fear of thinking that people will see me as stupid if I didn't get the answer correct and fear that I would be laughed at by my classmates. It was FEAR! FEAR!! FEAR!!! Fear made me a prisoner of my own self. Instead of expecting the best positive results from things, I was expecting the worst. Because I allowed this to control my mind, I became a captive of that enemy called FEAR.

On the other hand, *'If we make a conscious effort to expect the best, see the positive side of each situation and keep reminding ourselves that we can handle more than we often think, we will find ourselves with much less fear to deal with. Even if feelings of fear do manage to creep into our consciousness, we will still be able to keep them in perspective and balance then against an underlying sense of confidence.'* (Fearless motivation)

God has given us His spirit and is not a spirit of fear. 2 Timothy 1:7 says it all,

'For God has not given us a spirit of fear and timidity, but of power, love and self-discipline.'

God's desire is that we continually progress, that we reach higher heights and go to new levels. He doesn't want us to be captives because He has set us free from every form of captivity. He wants us to live always with Him free from every form of fear because He is a God who loves His people so much. Often, as soon as we make the decision to step out in faith and obey God, the enemy brings in fear to try to stop us. Our enemy of course is the devil. He doesn't want us to walk towards God. For God's plan for us to be accomplished, we will need to have faith in Him and put all our trust in Him. Faith connects us to God, but fear disconnects us from Him. This separation is exactly what the enemy wants to achieve by using fear against us.

In terms of doing God's will, the enemy uses fear to dissuade us. One of the reasons we find ourselves not doing the will of God is because we are afraid. More especially, we fear man and circumstances more than we fear the Lord God. Joseph was one of those individuals in the scriptures that the enemy tried to use fear against, to stop him from doing the will of God. In Matthew chapter 1:18, when Joseph first got to know about the pregnancy of Mary, He was afraid of what the outcome would be if the news became public knowledge. In Matthew 1:19, scripture says,

'Because Joseph was a righteous man and did not want to expose her to public disgrace (because he was more afraid of what people would say or do to her), **he had in mind to divorce her quietly.**'

While he was still entertaining the fear of what may happen because of the present situation of things, in verse 20, God sent His angel to come and reassure him:

'But after he had considered this, an angel of the Lord appeared to him in a dream and said, "Joseph, son of David, do not be afraid to take Mary home as your wife, because what is conceived in her is from the Holy Spirit."'

The enemy also uses fear against us whenever we want to make progress. At such moments, he will project thoughts into our minds like, what if you fail? What are people going to think about this? You know you don't have what it takes, and you are not good enough to do that, etc. He will do his best to use fear to try to convince us to hold back and stay where we are. If we allow him, he will feed us with his lies and then we will be filled with fear. We must never allow fear to dictate our decisions, because every time we do, fear increases and gains more of a stronghold on us.

Once fear sets in, faith gradually disappears. This is what kills our dreams. Do you know the number one killer of dreams, the number one reason why many people fail to live the life that they want to live, the number one reason why people fail to succeed, the number one reason why people try to run away from doing God's will? It is surely not just lack of money, opportunity, or the right circumstances, it is rather FEAR! But when faith is alive, we can stay focused on our dreams and refuse to give up, no matter the circumstances. We pursue our dreams with faith so that we will see them realised.

'The scripture makes it clear that fear is a spirit (2 Timothy 1:7). It plays on our emotions and holds us back. But the good news is that we have power over fear. The scripture says that perfect love

casts out all our fears. When we receive God's perfect love, we will have confidence about the future because we know that His plans are for our good'.

(Joel Osteen)

When we are fully aware of the fact that He is always in charge of whatever goes on in our lives, then we don't need to fear, we only need to trust and obey. When we are aware that He is the unchangeable changer who changes every situation but remains unchanged, then we don't need to listen to the lies of the devil.

Most often, what we are afraid of does not actually exist. That is why fear is simply *False Evidence Appearing Real*. Just know that fear is nothing but a lie. Let us therefore choose to believe God's word and receive His love so that we overcome fear and live a life of faith.

Are you living your fears instead of your dreams?

Is fear making you shy away from doing God's will for you?

Are you helpless and hopeless about this situation?

You don't need to be, just run to God; there is no hopeless situation in His sight. Go to His words in the scriptures and saturate your mind with them. His words will transform your mind and will build up your confidence and faith in Him, and then fear will bow out

(Romans 12:2).

Prayer:

Father, I thank you for taking me to new levels. I know you have equipped me with a spirit of power, love, and sound mind. Thank you for your confidence as I renounce fear and press forward to victory in Jesus' name, Amen.

Scriptures for study: *Psalm 56,3; 55:22; 27:1; 46:1; 34:7; Philippians 4:6-7, Isaiah 41:10, Mark 6:50; Deuteronomy 3:22; 1 Peter 5:6-7.*

10
Empty Your Life of Negativity

We used to have a funny lecturer back in my seminary days. One day he made a joke about some seminarians who were in the habit of staying away from activities in the seminary. (Seminarians are those studying for the priesthood). He said that some of them when they wake up in the morning, will start looking for an excuse why they shouldn't get out of bed and face the challenges of the day. He said either they start touching different parts of their body to see if there is any little pain or they invent one themselves. This is just to find a reason why they won't join in any activities for the day. They begin the day on a negative note, and that becomes how the whole day continues for them.

Often, we fill our lives with a lot of negativities with the result that we find it difficult to enjoy the happiness and peace which God desires for us. Once we open our hearts to negative thoughts, our doors are open to negative people, and surely, we will be troubled, and our lives will know no peace. John 14:1 tells us not to let our hearts become troubled. So, we must resolutely push negativity out of our lives.

I have come to realise that whenever my heart is filled with negative thoughts, I can never be happy and peaceful. It affects every aspect of my life – spiritually because I can't have a proper relationship with God, especially in prayer; physically because I can't eat properly, and I lose my appetite; psychologically because I can't think straight; emotionally because I want to be on my own and don't want to relate with anyone. This is not the way a human being would like to live.

Do you want a heart free from trouble? Do you want to live a happy life even when things are not working out the way you want? Then you must empty your life of negative thoughts and negative people, they are poison to your mind and heart. You don't need such thoughts in your life; you don't need such people in your life. We must learn to think every day of things that build positivity into our lives and not the things that will bring us down.

God wants to fill our hearts with peace, joy, and happiness. He wants us to be filled with His good things. But we must empty our lives of any form of negativity. This is because when our lives become filled with anger, jealousy, regrets, worries, insecurity, doubts, bitterness, etc, then there will be no space for the good things God wants to fill us with.

Stop proclaiming that you are not good enough and start saying you are specially made by God. Stop saying you can't be healed and start believing that you are healed by His stripes. Even if your sickness has been pronounced terminal and it seems there is no hope for you, remember there is no hopeless case for God, there is nothing impossible for Him because He says in Jeremiah 32:27,

'I am the God of all flesh, is there anything too hard for me.'

He is the specialist for impossible cases. Whose report will you believe the doctor's or God's? Remember, God has the final say and it is only what He says that stands. So instead of thinking how big your problem is, think of how big your God is. Instead of saying negative things about yourself, start bringing positivity into your life by the things you say and think about yourself.

You must be careful what you listen to, who you listen to and what you look at. Listen to things that uplift your and not things that bring you down in spirit. You don't need to keep sticking to the person that never says anything positive to you or about you. Let him or her go, you don't need them in your life. Some people are in the habit of putting others down for what they say. They do not want to see anything good about you; they do not want to see you rise above where you are. These are toxic people; they are like a cancer to the body. Once you give them that opportunity, they will keep growing and spreading to every part of your life and gradually and you will keep going down and down. The only way to prevent this cancerous spread of toxic people in your life is to cut them off completely. I know it may be very difficult to do this and that is why we need to call upon God for His grace, mindful that:

'... cut off from him we can do nothing'

(John 15:5)

Empty yourself of negative things and let God fill you with His good things.

We need to focus more on the positive side of life and less on the negative. When we are more focused on the negative aspects of life, it becomes very difficult to see the things to be thankful for in our lives. A grateful heart will always be a positive heart. The more we become grateful for everything, the more positive we will be in all things of life. If you are only grateful when things go right, you are negative. If you are grateful for everything that already is (including the unpleasant school of life lessons), then you can invite more and more positive energy into your life. Gratitude is positive. Instead of wasting energy focusing on the negative side of life, we should direct it towards the positive things. If we open our eyes we will see that there are a lot of things in our lives to be grateful for. That is a positive attitude to life. I will conclude this chapter from a story I heard from a friend:

'One day, a lecturer entered the lecture room and wanted to teach his students a lesson about life. He told his students to bring out their writing materials for an assessment. The students were taken aback because they were not prepared for the assessment. But then the lecturer assured them that he didn't need any of them to be prepared in order to do the assessment, all he wanted them to do was to look at a piece of paper and then follow the instructions he was going to give to them. When they were ready, the lecturer gave each of them a piece of paper with a black dot at the centre. Then he asked them to write something about the piece of paper he had just given to them. At the end when he collected the papers and went through what his students had written, he discovered that they had all concentrated on the black dot,

describing its position, size, etc. Then he taught them a lesson they will always remember. He told them that he observed that they were all so focused on the black dot at the centre of the paper that none of them noticed the whiteness of the paper. Then he said to them, "This is exactly what happens most often in life. We tend to focus so much more on the dark side of life (the negative things that happen to us and are around us) that we do not notice the many good things that have happened to us and the positive things that surround us."'

This is indeed true. When we focus on the negative side of life, then it becomes difficult for us to appreciate the fact that there are so many good things that life has to offer us. The same thing applies to human beings. If we are only interested in seeing the dark side of people, then it will be difficult for us to see the goodness in them no matter how small it may be. No one is 100% bad; there is still an element of goodness in each one of us. The God of all goodness created us all, and in one way or another, we reflect the goodness of our creator. He created us to be good, but often, we choose to be bad of our own free will. We have a gracious God who is loving and merciful beyond measure! He loves each person so much that He chooses to look beyond our dark side. He does not love our darkness, but he loves us, and He is willing to meet us where we are. He wants us to be happy. He puts out His hand to lead us out of negativity. There is an abundance of hope for everyone in God if we turn to Him. We should therefore ask God to help us and give us the grace to always focus more on living positively and to reject all negativity.

Prayer:
Heavenly Father, free me of every stronghold that prevents my smile. Sadness, discouragement, despair, lack of hope, misery, pain, hurt, anger and misfortune fall away at the sound of your great name. Lift my spirit, oh wonderful saviour, take control! *Amen.*

(Christianstt.com)

Scripture passages that can help you let go of negative thought: These are all from English Standard version of the Bible (ESV)

1 Peter 5:7 : *Casting all your anxieties on him, because he cares for you.*

Ephesians 4:26 : *Be angry and do not sin; do not let the sun go down on your anger,*

2 Timothy 1:7 : *For God gave us a spirit not of fear but of power and love and self-control.*

Philippians 4:13 : *I can do all things through him who strengthens me.*

Philippians 4:6 : *Do not be anxious about anything, but in everything by prayer and supplication with thanksgiving let your requests be made known to God.*

Luke 10:19 : *Behold, I have given you authority to tread on serpents and scorpions, and over all the power of the enemy, and nothing shall hurt you.*

Jeremiah 33:3 :*Call to me and I will answer you and will tell you great and hidden things that you have not known.*

Proverbs 3:5-6 : *Trust in the LORD with all your heart, and do not lean on your own understanding. In all your ways acknowledge him, and he will make straight your path.*

Let Go of the Past

I will begin this chapter with this lovely Zen story about letting go of the past.

'One day, two monks set out for a temple in a valley beyond the woods. While cutting a pathway through the woods, they came across a choppy stream they needed to cross. There, standing by the bank of the stream, was a beautiful young maiden dressed in silk. She was clearly at a loss as to how to cross without getting muddy and wet.

So, without thinking twice, the elder monk gestured to pick her up. Shocked, she obliged. He put her over his shoulder and waded across to the other side. The younger monk, dismayed and uneasy at what he had witnessed, followed in tow.

Upon reaching the other side of the bank, the elder monk put the maiden down gently. The maiden paid her respects and walked on. The monks then continued their journey to the temple.

As they navigated the forest, the younger monk, still troubled by what he'd seen, asked, "How could you do that? We aren't even supposed to make eye contact with women, let alone pick them up and carry them!"

Without a thought, the elder monk turned to the younger monk and said, "Oh, are you still carrying her? I put her down when I reached the other side of the stream."

And with that, the elder monk turned and continued leading the way through the forest, leaving the younger monk to contemplate his words for the remainder of the journey.'

We can see from this story how the older monk left everything that happened behind and continued his journey with happiness and satisfaction having done what he felt was right and good for his spiritual life. But the other monk remained stuck in the moment of what had just happened. While the older monk continued growing in his spiritual life because he let go, the younger monk suffered spiritual stagnation because he couldn't let go of the past.

This is exactly what happens in real life when we refuse to let go of things of the past. Sometimes we think holding on makes us strong, but it is letting go that does that. Letting go of the past is not very easy, we need courage and grace to be able to achieve it. But we gain a lot when we do achieve it. It was Deepak Chopra who said,

'In the process of letting go, you will lose many things from the past, but you will find yourself.'

In letting go, you will lose anxiety, pain, regret, and suffering, and what will be left is your improved self.

I am fully aware that to let go is not one of the easiest things to do, but it is one of the most beneficial things we can do for ourselves. Simon Heighweya, has this to say in his short write-up about letting go:

'I have realized that the reason I am suffering, stuck, in pain, and paralyzed, is the fact that despite talking, telling, teaching, and writing about 'letting go', I don't actually do it!'

I now have to let go of:
The past
My attachment to parents, family, friends
My false self, old self, ego
Attachment to memories, events, places
Fear, even the fear of letting go
Guilt
Blame
Shame

The label/fact of being adopted
Doubt
The known ideas of security
Other people's opinions of me,
Judgments about me
My own judgments
Some core false beliefs about myself and life
My conditioning by and attachment to the world
My defences
The future.

There are other experiences that can make someone become a captive of his or her own self. This is what living in the past can bring about. Living in the past is a problem because it robs you of the opportunity to enjoy the present. Not enjoying the present? If you aren't happy where you are, living in the past won't help! Living in the past causes you to avoid dealing with issues in the present. We must not allow yesterday's actions to affect today's progress, because letting go is necessary to truly thrive, otherwise we will always be afraid to face the future.

'Letting yesterday affect today will only destroy the excitement of tomorrow,'

(Michelle Cruz-Rosado)

The past is past and remains so. No matter how you think about it, the past can't return. So, the best thing is to accept that the past is no more. If there was a mistake made in the past, you can only work towards correcting it and making sure that you don't repeat it. We do not heal the past by dwelling there, we heal the past by living fully in the present. If you keep on remembering it and you allow it to rob you of the happiness of today and the excitement of tomorrow, you are treating yourself unfairly. Mandy Hale says,

'To get over the past, you first have to accept that the past is over. No matter how many times you revisit it, analyse it, regret it, or sweat it...it's over. It can hurt you no more.'

Our relationship with God can also be affected when we continue to live in the past. It is because of this that He told us in Isaiah 43:18-19,

> **'Forget the former things, do not dwell on the past. See, I am doing a new thing! Now it springs up, do you not perceive it?'**

Now the past becomes like a cataract in the eye; for as long as we continue to dwell in the past, we can't see the bright future which God has prepared for us. The past becomes a noisy background to what God is saying. We will see God talking to us, but we can't really hear what He is saying. I can remember some time ago when we went out to eat in one of the restaurants in town, the noise there was so loud that we couldn't hear what we were saying to each other. People were shouting at the top of their voices to be heard. We had to take our food away because we couldn't bear it. Once we left the noisy room, we were able to hear each other without stress.

Even if we have had an ugly past, God wants to heal our past and give us a better future. He speaks to us words of comfort that will help heal our wounded hearts. But the past can become for us a noisy background that makes it impossible to hear these soothing words.

It was Amit Ray who said that,

'If you want to fly in the sky, you need to leave the earth. If you want to move forward, you need to let go of the past that drags you down.'

Dwelling on the past is like someone climbing a mountain carrying many loads on his or her back. He or she can't make any progress because of the weight. But once he or she lets go of that weight, whatever it may be, his or her movement will become swift and a journey which would have been impossible to complete, will then become possible. The past, therefore, is like a heavy weight upon our back which makes our progress in life very difficult and most often impossible. But once we let go, then our progress will become speedy.

We should always be mindful of the fact that God has a plan for us. Jeremiah 29:11 reads,

> **'"For I know the plans I have for you," declares the LORD, "plans to prosper you and not to harm you, plans to give you hope and a future"'.**

Can you hear what God is saying to you at this moment? He said His plan is to give you and I, hope and a future. He is interested in our future, not our past. And if we wish to enjoy whatever He has planned for us in the future, then we must let go of the past. We can't hold firm to the past and expect to get anything in the future.

I want us to look at the following scriptural passages which are promises God made to His people. Let us see if they contain something in common that will give us the conviction that God deals with the future and not past, especially when it doesn't have anything good to offer. But first, we need to remember one thing; the past will always have a lesson to teach us. Albert Einstein once said,

> *'Learn from yesterday, live for today, hope for tomorrow.'*

God's word in the scripture has these to say to us about letting go of the past.

'You will indeed go out with joy and be led forth in peace; the mountains and hills will burst into song before you, and all the trees of the field will clap their hands.'

(Isaiah 55:12)

'"As for you, my servant Jacob, do not be afraid", declares the LORD, "and do not be dismayed, O Israel; for I will surely deliver you out of a distant place, your descendants from the land of their captivity! Jacob will return to quiet and ease, with no one to frighten him."'

(Jeremiah 30:10)

'This is what the LORD says: "I will restore the fortunes of Jacob's tents and have compassion on his dwellings. And the city will be rebuilt on her own ruins, and the palace will stand in its rightful place."'

(Jeremiah 30:18)

'"So there is hope for your future", declares the LORD, "and your children will return to their own land."'

(Jeremiah 31:17)

'Therefore, declare that this is what the Lord GOD says: 'Although I sent them far away among the nations and scattered them among the countries, yet for a little while I have been a sanctuary for them in the countries to which they have gone.'"

(Ezekiel 11:16)

'There I will give back her vineyards and make the Valley of Achor into a gateway of hope. There she will respond as she did in the days of her youth, as in the day she came up out of Egypt.'

(Hosea 2:15)

'So now I have resolved to do good again to Jerusalem and Judah. Do not be afraid.'

(Zechariah 8:15)

'This third I will bring through the fire; I will refine them like silver and test them like gold. They will call on my name, and I will answer them. I will say, "They are My people," and they will say, "The LORD is our God."'

(Zechariah 13:9)

Now can you see that there is something very common to all these passages above? They are all talking about the future by using the present tense "Will". When God says, "I will", it depicts certainty. He is not a man who can disappoint or fail when He makes a promise. Numbers 23:19 (KJV) says,

'God is not a man, that he should lie; neither the son of man, that he should repent: hath he said, and shall he not do it? or hath he spoken, and shall he not make it good?'

We must therefore ask God to help us and give us the courage to break up completely with the past, so that we can enjoy the present and enter the future full of excitement and expectations.

Prayer:

Dear God,

I let go of my need to be perfect, and I let You fill me with Your perfect love.

I let go of my ideas of fulfillment, and I let You fill me with what I truly desire.

I let go of what I think of myself, and I let You define my worth.

I let go of what others think of me, and I let You tell me who I am to You.

I let go of my appearance, and I let You shine through me.

I let go of my unreasonable standards, and I let You work through me.

I let go of my will for my life, and I let You reveal Your plan for me.

I let go of all my past sins, and I let You forgive me.

I let go of my reliance on myself, and I let You be my Redeemer.

I let go of how I view others, and I let You love them through me.

Amen

Kate Prain

12
He is Not Interested in Your Past

There was this lovely man I used to visit in my former parish who was housebound. I visited him for almost a year and from time to time, he requested me to hear his confession. I observed that normally at the end of the confession, he didn't have the satisfaction of someone who had just confessed his sins and received forgiveness. Afterwards, he would say to me, "Father, I don't really believe God can forgive me because I did a lot of terrible things in the PAST." Each time I would keep assuring him that God is no longer interested in his past as long as he has confessed his sins and repented of them. I told him that all he needed to do was to accept in faith that his sins were forgiven and forgotten. He never told me what it was that he had done, and I was not really interested in finding out, but I kept on assuring him that God is no longer interested in what he has done previously. Whatever he did was no longer in His book because God does not keep records of our past lives, if we have reconciled with Him. The scripture says that once we confess and repent of our sins, no matter what they may be, the Precious Blood of Jesus cleanses all of us of our unrighteousness.

Every time I returned, he always said the same thing, as if he had never heard those reassuring words before. It was very disturbing because I know that even when God has forgiven us, it is left for us to accept His forgiveness in faith and to forgive ourselves. If this doesn't happen, then our relationship with Him will still be on shaky ground because we are not putting our trust in Him, rather we are allowing the enemy the opportunity to convince us that God can never forgive us. Consequently, our communication with God will be more difficult when we harbour doubts about whether He is listening to our prayers.

On my last visit to this man before he passed away, to the greater glory of God, before I left, he said to me, "Father, I believe that God has forgiven me." My heart was full of joy as I heard this from him. Before I left, he asked me to call his son for him which I did. As I was walking back home, I heard someone calling out my name. It was the man's son running after me, so I stopped. When he got to where I was standing, breathlessly he said,

"Father, I have been asked by my dad to tell you that he believes."

I smiled and told him that he already told me that before I left the house. It was my last encounter with this man after a year of weekly visits. He died two days after that visit. I was so happy that he had finally accepted God's forgiveness and let go of whatever had happened in the past that was preventing Him from enjoying God's promise of salvation for all.

Jeremiah 29:11 reminds us that God has a perfect plan for us. This means that God has a very wonderful future for us. If He is interested in blessing our future, it therefore also means that He can never be interested in our past if we have truly repented whatever has happened and promise never to go back to it anymore. The scripture says in 1 John 1:9,

'If we confess our sins, he is faithful and just and will forgive us our sins and purify us from all unrighteousness.'

It says here that He will purify, wash, and cleanse us of our dirty past. We only need to acknowledge (Jeremiah 3:13) and confess and forsake whatever we did wrong in the past. Once this is done, He forgives us, He chooses to forget it forever. Once we have been forgiven, whatever sin we committed ceases to exist before God. No cloth that is washed goes back to being dirty again with the exact same dirt that was washed from it. Once the dirt is washed from the cloth, the dirty water used is poured away and not seen again. When God washes away our sins they are gone from His sight forever. By the power of His Precious Blood our sinful past, no matter how dark it was, is made as white as snow once our sins are confessed and forsaken.

1 John 1:7 says,

'... and the blood of Jesus, His son, purifies us from all sin.'

This blood is so powerful it can purify even the greatest sinner on this earth.

'How does Jesus' blood purify us from every sin then? Going back to the Old Testament times, we observe that believers symbolically transferred their sins to an animal which they then sacrificed (see a description of this ceremony in Leviticus 4). The animals died in their place to pay for their sin and to allow them to continue living in God's favour. God graciously forgave them because of their faith in Him and because they obeyed the commandments concerning the sacrifice. Those sacrifices anticipated the day when Christ will completely remove sin. Real cleansing from sin came with Jesus, 'the Lamb of God who takes away the sin of the world.' (1 John 1:29.) Sin by its very nature brings death - that is a fact as certain as the Law of Gravity. Jesus did not die for His own sins; He had none. Instead, by a transaction that we may never fully understand, he died for the sins of the world. When we commit our lives to Christ and thus identify ourselves with Him, His death becomes ours. He has paid the penalty for our sins, and His blood has purified us. Just as Christ rose from the grave, we rise to a new life of fellowship with him (Romans 6:4)'

(Commentary from Application Bible)

Now let me bring it to your mind again, *'God is not interested in your past.'*

I can hear someone asking, "How can God forget my past? Do you know what I have done? Do you know how badly I have treated my parents? Do you know I have always been an addict of drugs, alcohol, sex, porn, etc.? Do you know how many times I have committed myself to have an abortion? Do you know that I have done this or that in the past? So how can you say that God is not interested in my past?

I repeat again:

'Beloved, God Our Loving Father is not interested in your past'

If God was interested in our past, then the future would not make sense. Our God is a God of new life and new beginnings. The scriptures in 2 Cor 5:17 say,

'If anyone is in Christ, he/she is a new creation, old things have passed away, behold all things have become new.'

When God says you are 'a new creation' He means that, *'God who created all things through Christ has restored his work, deformed by sin, by re-creating it in Christ'*

(Jerusalem Bible footnote 5f)

You have a new heart, a new personality, a new life in Christ. Anything that characterised the old nature, personality, etc., has passed away. He is not interested in who you used to be. He is interested in who you are now. He is not interested in what you used to do. He is interested in what you are doing right now.

Yes, God forgets our past, for He has forgiven us of all the mean, low-down things we have done. Our past has gone in God's eyes; instead, we have a great future in eternity. Isn't that an amazing thing to hear?

No matter how dirty our past may be, God can still wipe it clean if only we can humble ourselves and ask for forgiveness;

'If my people, who are called by my name, will humble themselves and pray and seek my face and turn from their wicked ways, then I will hear from heaven, and I will forgive their sin and will heal their land.'

(2 Chronicles 7:14)

It doesn't matter what we think we have done in the past, however bad we may think we have acted or the way we have treated others, God invites us to come to Him just the way we are, and He will make us whole;

'Come now, let us settle the matter," says the LORD. "Though your sins are like scarlet, they shall be as white as snow; though they are red as crimson, they shall be like wool.'

If you are still doubting that God can forgive your past, then reflect on His promises. Believe that they are true and that they are for you. All you need to do is accept them in faith. They are for all of us. Carefully consider these promises from God's word:

'I yes, I am He, who blots out your transgressions for My own sake and remembers your sins no more.'

(Isaiah 43:25)

'I have blotted out your transgressions like a cloud, and your sins like a mist. Return to Me, for I have redeemed you.'

(Isaiah 44:22)

'The One who vindicates Me is near. Who will dare to contend with Me? Let us confront each other! Who has a case against me? Let him approach Me!'

(Isaiah 50:8)

'Let the wicked man forsake his own way and the unrighteous man his own thoughts; let him return to the LORD, that He may have compassion, and to our God, for He will freely pardon.'

(Isaiah 55:7)

'But if a wicked man turns from the wickedness he has committed and does what is just and right, he will save his life.'

(Ezekiel 18:27

'None of the sins he has committed will be held against him. He has done what is just and right; he will surely live.'

Ezekiel 33:16)

Today, don't let anybody remind you who you were. Don't allow your past, whatever it may be, to hold you down so that you can't cry out to the Master for forgiveness. God wants you to move on. He is ever patiently waiting for our return just like the father in the story of the Prodigal Son, God is always excited to see His lost son or daughter return to Him. (Luke 15:11-32). He is so excited it is as if He doesn't even remember that we have a past. If God, who we offend through our sinfulness is always excited to have us back, then nothing should stop us from returning to Him.

We need to remember that the only reason Jesus came to die on the cross, was for our sins to be cleansed. He wanted to restore us to new life in Him. Therefore, if there is any sin too big for His blood to cleanse or wash away, it would mean that His death was pointless. The good news is that His blood is powerful enough to blot out every possible sin completely.

No matter how bad your past looks, or how vile you think it was, if you are in Christ, you are a new creation. Your past doesn't define you. Despite all the failures and whatever mistakes, you think you have made in your life, you are a new creation, and your past is history. True change comes when you make a clear cut between your past and present. You will experience true peace when you stop beating yourself up for what you did and start enjoying the gift of God that is available through Jesus Christ. If God can let go of your past, you should do the same. In Isaiah 43:25 the Lord says:

'I, even I, am he who blots out your transgressions for my own sake and remembers your sins no more.'

Prayer: Prayer for Forgiveness, (from the Bible, Psalm 51.)

Please have mercy on me, O Lord, according to your unfailing love. According to your great compassion block out my transgressions. Wash away all my failures and cleanse me from my sins. For I know my transgressions and my sins are always with me.

Against You, and only You have I sinned and done what is evil in Your sight.

Father, You are right in your conclusion and justified when You judge. Surely, I was sinful at birth, sinful from the time my mother conceived me. Yet, You desired faithfulness even in the womb; You taught me wisdom in that secret place.

Father, cleanse me with hyssop, and I will be clean. Wash me, and I will be whiter than snow. Let me hear joy and gladness. Let the bones you have crushed rejoice. Lord, hide your face from my sins and block out all my iniquity.

Make in me a pure heart, Heavenly Father, and renew a steadfast spirit inside me.

Do not remove me from your presence or take your Holy Spirit from me. Restore to me the joy of your salvation and give me a willing spirit, to sustain me.

Then I will teach the lost your ways, so that sinners will turn back to you.

Deliver me from the guilt of bloodshed, O Lord, You are God my Saviour, and my tongue. I will sing of your righteousness. Open my lips, Lord, and my mouth will declare your praise.

Amen.

(Psalm 51.)

Bible verses for putting the past behind you: *1 John 1:9, Philippians 3:13-14, Isaiah 43:18-19, Galatians 2:20-21, Matthew 6:15, Acts 2:38, 2 Cor 5:17-18,*

13
Pressed, But Not Crushed

On 19th December 2004, I had a very bad accident. As a result, I endured terrible pain accompanied by temptation and trials. I began to see a deep meaning in some scriptural passages at that time, and they helped me to see meaning in all that was happening to me within this period. One of those passages was that of St Paul's second letter to the Corinthians chapter 4: 8-9 which reads:

'We are hard pressed on every side, but not crushed; perplexed, but not in despair, persecuted, but not abandoned; struck down but not destroyed.'

There came a point when the 'why me' question was constantly on my lips. The pain I was going through became too much, it was practically unbearable. The thought that my friends were all in school while I was stuck at home made me want to lose my head. The temptation to give up on God and my vocation was strong because I kept getting that feeling that I may not actually recover enough to go back to school. But amid all this pressure, I was constantly reassured by God that I would not be crushed. I was reassured through His word, especially 2 Corinthians 4:8-9 (quoted already above), and Psalm 34:1

'Many are the afflictions of the righteous, but God delivers him out of them all',

and Romans 8:18

'I consider that our present sufferings are not worth comparing with the glory that will be revealed in us.'

These passages kept me going when I almost lost it.

One of the questions that kept coming into my head was, "God why should you allow me to be suffering this way and be afflicted with these painful trials when I have decided to answer your call to become your priest?"

Why are we pressed? Why is it that we must be pressed (undergo trials, temptations, persecutions, sufferings of different kinds, etc), even when we are faithful to God?

In Acts 14:22, the word of God says,

'... strengthening the disciples and encouraging then to remain true to the faith. "We must go through many hardships to enter the kingdom of God."'

But why on earth do we need to be pressed?

I was trying to find answers to all these questions when the Lord led me to the book of Job, and I carefully read through all the chapters. I would also advise you to make time to read this book of the Bible if you have found yourself asking God anything like the same questions that I found myself asking of Him then. The story of Job helped me to understand better what St Paul meant when he said that,

'We are hard pressed on every side but not crushed.'

It therefore gave me the assurance that even though I was experiencing this hard pressure at this time, I was not going to be crushed, rather, I would come out refined. It became very clear to me that God only allowed me to be pressed for a reason. Any spiritual growth that takes place in our life will always be accompanied by the trials of life.

'He knows the way that I take, when He has tested me, I will come forth as gold.'

(Job 23:10)

We shouldn't get this wrong; God is not a sadist who wants to see His beloved children crushed. He wants us to know that we can never exist independently of Him. He only allows us to be pressed because in such moments, with our whole trust and hope in Him, He will make all things work for our good.

(Romans 8:28).

I remember my mum taught us at a young age how to produce palm oil from palm fruit. First, the palm fruit must be red, which shows it is ripe and ready. Then it is cut down and all the fruit is removed from the bunch. The fruit is then boiled at a high temperature. After that, it is crushed with a mortar and then, finally, pressed in a machine. It's only at this time that the oil in the fruit will come out. It's not an easy process but there is always hope that the process leads to something, the precious oil.

There is 'precious oil' within each one of us. Even if we can't see it ourselves and neither can others, God sees it in us. But for this precious oil (this gift, talent, potential) to be produced, we need to be pressed. All the trials, temptations, difficulties and all the painful things that come to us, are the way we are being pressed to cause that 'precious oil' to come out. But these troubles and tribulations are not always coming against us. They come only when we are ripe to produce the oil in us. No one enjoys suffering, but God is saying to you, "I am pressing you, but not crushing you. I am pressing you because of the precious oil in you." God knows that there is precious oil in me and you and thus He allows us to be pressed to bring out that oil. But one thing we can be sure of is that He will not crush us or allow us to be crushed the way the palm fruit is crushed to produce the palm oil. God is always full of love, mercy and compassion for us. He only allows our suffering because He can see the greater good will come of it, for all of us, 'precious oil.'

One thing we should be mindful of in our lives as Christians, is that there is no assurance that it will be free from difficulties, pain or sorrows. So, we shouldn't be surprised or perplexed when such things begin to happen in our lives. Our brother St Peter's, advice to us in 1 Peter 4:12-16,

'Dear friends, do not be surprised at the painful trial you are suffering, as though something strange were happening to you. But rejoice that you participate in the suffering of Christ, so that you may be overjoyed when his glory is

reviewed. If you are insulted because of the name of Christ, you are blessed, for the spirit of glory and God rests on you.'

Instead of being perplexed, St James says to us,

'Consider it pure Joy, my brethren, whenever you face trials of many kinds, because you know that the testing of your faith develops perseverance. Perseverance must finish its work so that you may be mature and complete not lacking anything.'

(James 1:2-4)

There is no assurance that the children of God will be free from pressing of any kind, the only assurance is that there will be no crushing if we trust in Him who alone is worthy and has the power to deliver us safely.

In Isaiah 43:1-2, the scripture says,

'But now, this is what the Lord says- he who created you O Jacob, he who formed you O Israel. Fear not, for I have redeemed you; I have summoned you by name, you are mine. When you pass through the waters, I will be with you and when you pass through the rivers, they will not sweep over you. When you walk through the fire, you will not be burned; the flames will not set you ablaze.'

As we can see in this passage, it didn't say "if you pass through the waters," which is conditional, rather it says, "*when* you pass through the waters", which is definite. By using the word 'when,' it shows us there will be a time when we will cross the river. So, there is no assurance that because we are children of God, crossing the river will not be our portion, as some preachers would have us believe. At one point or another in our lives, we will certainly have a river to cross. It may be the river of sickness, loss of a loved one, loss of a job, family problems and pressures, depression, betrayal, or another kind of suffering. But just like the psalmist in Psalm 34 says, the Lord will deliver us from it all if we trust and hope in Him.

So, the assurance here is that we will not be drowned. We will also go through fire and will not be burned. A wise old man was approached by another man one day, who told him that he was passing through hell. The wise old man's reply was,

'My son, it is good you are passing through hell, but remember you must keep going through and don't stay in hell.'

Listen to this, there are 3 facts about your life as a Christian: First, you can be sure, you will have troubles. Secondly, you can be sure, that God will deliver you from trouble. Thirdly, you can be sure you can become free of your troubles. We can be knocked down by troubles, but with God in charge, we cannot be knocked out. We will surely stand up again, and this time, we will be stronger than before.

Prayer:

O God, you know our hearts and you know how fragile we can be, particularly in the crucible of suffering when we don't understand why, in your hard providence, we endure what we endure.

And in those moments, we acknowledge that the temptation to distort the truth is very real, to misunderstand, to accuse You or to twist reality or the truth of your word to fit our circumstances. Or to omit vital truth, to overly simplify and perhaps even at times collapse into despair.

Help us, please, to learn instead the difficult path, to walk the difficult path of submission in faith, trusting the living God who leads us through the valley of the shadow of death. For we ask it in Jesus' name,

Amen.

(Culled from, 'I shall come forth as Gold.' by David Strain)

Chapter 14
Who do You Go to in Times like These?

A friend once sent me something that inspired me to write on this theme and I want to use it to begin this topic:

"Where do you keep your problems?

If you keep your problems in your head, you will run mad.

If you keep your problems in your heart, you will have a heart attack.

If you keep your problems in your mouth, you will become talkative.

If you keep your problems in your house, you will have a broken home.

If you keep your problems to yourself, you will die with them.

If you keep your problems with your colleagues, they may create more problems for you.

If you ignore your problems, you will be prolonging the evil days.

If you disclose your problems to your friends, you may be mocked.

If you share your problems with your family, you may be disrespected.

If you keep your problems in your face, you may look ugly.

If you keep your problems in your bed, you may have nightmares.

If you take your problems to school, you will surely fail.

If you take your problems to Satan, you will surely regret it.

Hand over your problems to God, casting all your fears upon Him for he cares for you"

There are times in life when things become so unbearable that it can seem like everything around us is turning against us, and that the dependable people we expect to be there for us are nowhere to be found. At this point, we tend to become confused and don't know what to do or who to run to. When such times occur, who do you run to? Do you give up on life and God so easily? This is the time when our faith is put to the test.

When we are hit by the storms of life, we are most likely to turn to people who are close to us who we believe will help alleviate our pain. This is natural and very much encouraged. We were created to be there for each other. But there comes a point in life when we are so badly hit, that not even our family or friends can be of any help to us, sometimes even to the point that we see them giving up on us because they can't cope anymore. These are always very difficult moments in our lives, when we become so confused that we do not know who to turn to anymore. Have you experienced such moments?

What did you do and who did you run to?

As for me, at such moments, it is God that I run to, and He has never disappointed me. He even takes care of the problems that look impossible to resolve. I have never seen Him as my last resort, but always as my first point of call whenever I have needed help.

I believe the Psalmist experienced such a moment when there was practically no one to turn to except God. This led him to recount in Psalm 121: 1-2,

> *'I lift up my eyes to the hills. From where does my help come? My help comes from the LORD, the Maker of heaven and earth. He will not allow your foot to slip; your Protector will not slumber.'*

The story of Hannah in 1 Samuel 1:1-20, gives us a clear idea of what to do when such moments come. Remember, such moments will surely come, which is why we must always be ready. Life does not warn us before it hits us hard.

Hannah had been unable to conceive, and in Old Testament times, a childless woman was considered a failure. Her barrenness was a social embarrassment for her husband. Coming from a culture where children are believed to be a very important reason for marriage, I can imagine what Hannah was going through, not only in the hands of Peninnah, but also outsiders. In my culture, when a woman can't give her husband a child, she is in for big trouble. She will be called different derogatory names, she will be treated disrespectfully, and some will even begin to refer to her as a man living with a man. Worse still, if the family of the husband does not strongly support the marriage, they will do everything possible to upset the woman. After some time, the family will start pressuring the man to marry another woman. At that point, a lot of women become very confused and helpless. Many of them in such situations involve themselves in things they later regret. At this point, some of the wiser amongst them will run to God, but many don't know how to. No one who ran to God at such moments has ever been disappointed.

Part of God's plan for Hannah involved postponing her years of childbearing. While Peninnah and Elkanah looked at Hannah's outward circumstances, God was moving ahead with His plan. Do you hear this?

Even in the darkest moments of our lives, when people are looking down on us, God is moving ahead with His own plan for us.

Hannah knew her husband loved her, but even his encouragement could not comfort her. She could not keep from listening to Peninnah's jeers and letting Peninnah's words erode her self-confidence. Listen, although we cannot keep others from unjustly criticising us, we can choose how we will react to their hurtful words. Rather than dwelling upon our problems, we can enjoy the loving relationships God has given us. By so doing, we can exchange self-pity for hope.

Hannah had good reason to feel discouraged and bitter. She was unable to bear children; she shared her husband with a woman who ridiculed her; her loving husband could not solve her problem and even the high priest misunderstood her motives. But instead of retaliating or giving up hope, Hannah prayed. She brought her problem honestly before God. She went straight to, Him because she knew that He had the solution to her problem. She didn't go about wasting her tears, rather, she invested her tears in prayer to God.

1 Samuel 1:19 says,

'... **and the Lord remembered her**'

She conceived and gave birth to a son who she named Samuel. God changed her weeping into dancing, her tears of sorrow into tears of joy. God put a new song in her mouth.

Each of us may face times of bareness when nothing 'comes to birth' in our work, service, or relationships. It is difficult to pray in faith when we feel so ineffective. But, as Hannah discovered, prayer opens the way for God to work. So, my beloved one, instead of running up and down and falling into self-pity, go to God and unload your worries to Him. Remember He is always there waiting for you - in the Blessed Sacrament, at Mass, at prayer meetings, in your home, and in your heart. He wants you to feel free to always come to Him.

So, we must not forget that God is always there for us, and we can always run to Him, not just in times of trouble, but always.

'When you become tired and restless, run to God and you will find rest for your soul.

(Matthew 11:28)

Are you looking for a solution to your problem? Then you must run to Him and not from Him. We cannot be running away from the answer and at the same time hoping to get solutions to our problems. Even when we mess up, we still don't need to run away from God, but rather we should run to Him. He is always there waiting for us, in good times and in bad. He is our first and last, there at the beginning and the end. So, let us never hesitate to go to God. Let us always go to Him, not just when we are in need.

Prayer:

Thank You heavenly Father that Your mercies are new every morning and that Your faithfulness never fails.

Thank You that You are interested in every area of my life and that despite my many faults and failings You have promised to lead and to guide in all things.

And thank You Lord... that You have promised to supply the sufficient grace I need in every situation of my life. Father, as I seem to have come to a bit of a stand-still in my life, I pray for Your grace and guidance to lead and direct in the days that lie ahead.

You have promised to be with me and to go before me...so that if I turn to the right hand or to the left, I will hear a voice right behind me... guiding me... saying,

"This is the way; walk in it."

Give me Your grace and guidance in the choices I need to make in my life. Thank You Father that your grace is sufficient and that no matter where I go or what I do You have promised to be with me – thank You in Jesus name,

Amen.

(Knowing Jesus.com)

Scriptures about running to God in times of need: Psalm 71:1-24, Philippians 4:6-7, Psalm 55:22, 1 Peter 5:7, Romans 12:19, Matthew 11:28-30, Proverbs 3:5-6.

15
You are God's Masterpiece

'For we are God's handiwork, created in Christ Jesus to do good works, which God prepared in advance for us to do.'

(Ephesians 2:10)

Imagine the type of smile that radiates on the face of an artist after painting a very beautiful picture of something, or after carving a beautiful image of himself or someone else. The smile on their face shows their approval of the work they have done – that they are satisfied with it and see that it is good. It becomes their masterpiece. Whenever they look at the work of their own hand, it gives them joy.

In the same way, whenever God looks at you, He smiles. Do you know the reason? Simply because you are His masterpiece. You are specially made by God. You are a perfect representation of God's handiwork. It does not matter what your physical appearance maybe, what matters is that you represent the image of God himself. In Genesis 1:27 it is written,

'So, God created man in His own image, in the image of God he created him, male and female he created them.'

In what ways are we made in God's image? God obviously did not create us exactly like himself because God has no physical body. Instead, we are reflections of God's glory. Some feel that our reason, creativity, speech, or self-determination *is* the image of God. More likely it is our entire self that reflects the image of God. We will never be totally like God because he is our supreme creator, but we do have the ability to reflect his character in love, patience, forgiveness, kindness, and faithfulness.

Knowing that we are not only God's masterpiece but also made in His own image, and thus, share many of his characteristics, provides a solid basis for self-worth. Human worth is not based on possessions, achievements, physical attractiveness or public acclaim,

'And he said unto them, take heed, and beware of covetousness: for a man's life consisteth not in the abundance of the things which he possesseth.'

(L12:15, NKJV)

Instead, it is based on being made in God's image. Because we bear God's image, we can feel positive about ourselves. Criticising or downgrading ourselves, seeing ourselves as useless, wanting to change our colour or sex, etc., is criticising what God has made and the abilities he has given us.

I like what Connie Rowland wrote in her article; *you are God's Masterpiece*:

'It didn't happen suddenly or accidentally. The creative process was followed, and the work completed. It started with a blank canvas. The moment God spun the world into motion, His master plan began to take shape. The intimate details of your life were accounted for as He sketched the outline of your being, painted your portrait, and carefully feathered in the background. He poured Himself into you, and over time, created the masterpiece that is you.

It was a painstaking process. And the final brushstroke of pure genius came as the nails were driven into the Saviour's hands. It was the hard work of Jesus on the cross that made you a new being. He gave the very best of Himself that day, knowing you would emerge as His greatest masterpiece!'

Knowing that you are a person of worth helps you to love God, to know him personally, and to make a valuable contribution to those around you. It's only when you see yourself as worthless that you will not believe in yourself and in what you can achieve in this life. Because you are God's masterpiece, He has fully loaded you with great potential. But until you discover who you are in

God, until you discover how special you are in His eyes, and that you are the **'apple of His eye'** (Zachariah 2:8), until you come to realise how many blessings He has poured into your life as His child, then you will never know your true identity and you will not enjoy your inheritance as His child.

Let no one bring you down and never bring yourself down either, God has lifted you up by making you His masterpiece and that is what you are, anything below that, is not permitted in your life.

May God continue to help us, and may He open our eyes to see and appreciate the great masterpiece that He has made of us.

Prayer:
Gracious God, this news is almost too good to be true. I am your handiwork, your masterpiece! Amazing! Almost too amazing for me to believe. I am so aware, Lord, of my foibles and failings.

As it ages, my body reminds me how far I am from any sort of physical masterpiece. And you know the ways I miss the mark in my actions and in my soul. Yet, I am a masterpiece, not because of my effort, but because of your grace.

How I thank you for what you have begun to do in me through Christ.

May I see myself in light of this truth.

May I live each day embodying this truth.

May I be your masterpiece today, Lord, in all I do, think, say, and feel.

Amen.

(Culled from 'You Are God's Masterpiece', Daily Reflection:
Produced by 'The High Calling')

Afterword

God is always there for us, he communicates with us in the right way and at the right time, especially at our most difficult times of need. He hears our cries, He lifts us up, He shows us how to let go of our burdens and He forgives us always. Fear, negativity and pressure will always be obstacles in the way as we continue our journey through life, but God will always show us the way to overcome them. Each one of us is His 'Masterpiece of creation', equipped to deal with anything life throws at us, as long as we open our hearts and follow His ways.

I hope this book has shown you some clear pathways to take going forward with your journey of faith. We look forward to the second volume of *A Fountain of Hope*, which, by God's grace will be coming your way soon.

Follow us on our social media platforms:

TikTok @voiceofhopefamily, **Facebook**/Voice of hope family, **YouTube** Ibeh Alvan, Voice of hope family, **Instagram,** Voice of_hope_family.

God bless you.

Fr. Alvan Ibeh, SMMM

About the Author

Fr Alvan Ibeh, SMMM belongs to a religious order known as *The Sons of Mary Mother of Mercy Congregation* founded by a Nigerian Bishop, the late Anthony Gogo Nwedo, CSSP. He was ordained a Priest on the 21st of July 2012 and is working as a missionary in the Catholic Diocese of East Anglia, England.

Apart from working in the Parish, Fr Alvan is also a hospital and school Chaplain. He Started a group, named *Voice of Hope Family*, which is aimed at gathering young talented men and women who through music and other gifts will help bring the message of hope to our world of today.

BV - #0110 - 290724 - C0 - 210/148/5 - PB - 9780992957391 - Gloss Lamination